# Turn on the Lights—
# From Bed!

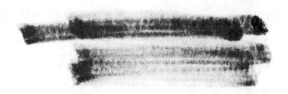

Also by Robert S. Carrow
*Put a Fan in Your Hat!*

# Turn on the Lights— From Bed!

## Inventions, Contraptions, and Gadgets Kids Can Build

Robert S. Carrow

Illustrations by Rick Brown

**LEARNING TRIANGLE PRESS**

*Connecting
kids, parents, and teachers
through learning*

**An imprint of McGraw-Hill**

New York  San Francisco  Washington, D.C.  Auckland  Bogotá  Caracas
Lisbon  London  Madrid  Mexico City  Milan  Montreal  New Delhi
San Juan  Singapore  Sydney  Tokyo  Toronto

# McGraw-Hill

## A Division of The *McGraw·Hill* Companies

pbk    1 2 3 4 5 6 7 8 9   DOC/DOC   9 0 2 1 0 9 8 7 6
hc      1 2 3 4 5 6 7 8 9   DOC/DOC   9 0 2 1 0 9 8 7 6

**Library of Congress Cataloging-in-Publication Data** (applied for)
Carrow, Robert S.

ISBN 0-07-011659-8 (pbk)
ISBN 0-07-011656-3 (hc)

McGraw-Hill books are available at special quantity discounts to use as premiums and sales promotions, or for use in corporate training programs. For more information, please write to the Director of Special Sales, McGraw-Hill, 11 West 19th Street, New York, NY 10011. Or contact your local bookstore.

Acquisitions editor: Kimberly Tabor
Editorial team: Executive editor: Lori Flaherty
             Managing editor: Andrew Yoder
             Book editor: April Nolan
             Indexer: Jodi L. Tyler
Production team: DTP supervisor: Pat Caruso
             DTP operators: Kim Sheran, Tanya Howden
             DTP computer artist supervisor: Tess Raynor
             DTP computer artists: Nora Ananos, Charles Burkhour, Steve Gellert, Charles Nappa
Designer: Jaclyn J. Boone                                                SIES3

To my daughter Justine Marie Carrow,
who wanted to help with all the projects. Some were even her ideas.
May she and all children continue to create,
invent, and contribute. We **need** this from them!

# Contents

# Introduction
## *So you want to invent...*

**Yes, I said stop!** Don't skip ahead to the projects yet! This book can give you hours of fun and some really cool projects, but you're going to need a little help before you begin. So here it is.

## Profile of an inventor

If the shoe fits, wear it. In other words, if you think you could be an inventor, be one! All types of people can invent. There are educated inventors, absent-minded inventors, and lucky inventors (people who were in the right place at the right time). Those lucky inventors were not only in the right place at the right time—they also had the smarts to recognize an opportunity because they had their eyes and ears open. They were constantly on the lookout for ideas, components for their ideas, and opportunities to use their ideas. The inventor of the future (you?) has to be ready!

# Turn on the Lights—From Bed!

The following list describes qualities common to inventors. If you have at least five of these qualities, you're on your way to being an inventor yourself! How many do you have?

**1 Inventors are resourceful**
When inventors need a part or component, they find it. They believe it can be found or it can be done!

**2 Inventors are always thinking, and thinking ahead**
Whenever inventors have time to kill, they are thinking constructively by asking themselves questions about the world around them.

**3 Inventors are pack rats**
They collect anything and everything, knowing that someday, for some project, they might need that special something as part of an invention.

**4 Inventors take learning seriously**   An education can only help the young inventor know more. Knowing more can lead to more ideas!

**5 Inventors ask a lot of questions**   If they don't know why something works, they ask. Then they know!

**6 Inventors are adventurous**  Whenever someone is going to throw away an old appliance or device, inventors get it and take it apart. They might find a part they need or actually see how something works, but they know this can help them invent.

**7 Inventors read and write**  Famous inventors have to be able to read and write well. (They won't become famous if they can't document their work.) Reading can give you the basic understanding of practically everything. Whether you read books, magazines, or the newspaper, you are learning and getting ideas.

**8  Inventors doodle**
Another related skill inventors should have is the ability to sketch. If an inventor draws a picture of an invention ahead of time, he or she can work out problems on paper before wasting time and money on the actual project. But sketching is also good for those who are being shown what the invention can do.

**9  Inventors are patient**  If inventors weren't patient, they would go crazy when things didn't work. The saying, "If at first you don't succeed, try, try again," applies here.

**10  Inventors "mind exercise"**  Ask lots of questions. Wonder about everything! A healthy mind is a creative one.

Of course, there are no guarantees in life when it comes to success. But if you never try, you'll never succeed, either. Inventors are like explorers: They try new things, think of creative ways to solve problems, and basically have fun. You can be this person . . . and if you're reading this book, you *are* this person!

Whatever your reason to invent, always strive to make it fun and rewarding. Never invent under pressure. Give yourself plenty of time because you can absolutely count on running into surprises and obstacles along the way, and these will take time and thought to overcome.

Reading books about famous inventors can be helpful, too. Books about Benjamin Banneker, Marie Curie, Thomas Edison, Nikola Tesla, and other inventors and scientific pioneers will tell you about other young inventors and the way they lived. Get involved with science clubs. Visit your local science museum. Participate in science fairs and contests whenever you can. Don't worry about winning; just go to the fairs and observe who wins and with what projects.

## The inventor's challenge

You, as an inventor, have accepted a challenge: to solve a particular problem. Have you ever heard the saying, *necessity is the mother of invention*? It's a fancy way of saying that if you need something, you'll find a way to get it. Engineers, scientists, and inventors all create because they *need* something for some purpose.

Inventing—and, really, science in general—is about taking this need or problem and asking questions about *how* to solve it until you come up with a *way* to solve it. Sometimes a solution is not ideal because it's too expensive or it takes too long or it isn't practical. In that case, you need to keep asking questions until you come up with something that will solve the problem perfectly for you.

# Turn on the Lights—From Bed!

## Inventor M.O.
## (Modus Operandi, method of operation)

Once you have accepted the challenge to solve a problem, you need to develop a plan of attack. Start with paper and pencil (with an eraser, so that you can erase when you need to change something). Write at the top of the page the problem and the proposed solution. The solution is your goal. Next, list all the steps you could take to reach your goal. This list should include materials, procedures, and a sequence. Remember that you have to do the first things first!

Let's use the remote-control lights-on-from-bed project on the cover of the book as an example of this kind of scientific thought. You'll need to have a question-and-answer session with yourself, like this:

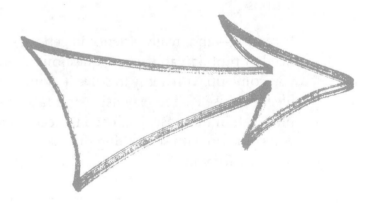

What's the <u>problem</u>?
I want to be able to turn my bedroom light on and off from the comfort of my bed, but I can't reach the switch!

What's the <u>solution</u>?
I could make a device that will turn the lights on and off for me.

How do I do <u>that</u>?
Well, I could make a long arm-like device that will reach from the bed to the light switch.

What's <u>wrong with that solution</u>?
It would probably be a little hard to control something that long, and I'd probably knock stuff over and poke holes in the wall.

What's a <u>better way to tackle the problem</u>?
I could create a remote-control device that would work with switches and wires - without destroying my room.

⭐ <u>In other words, turn on the lights - from bed!</u>

## Turn on the Lights–From Bed!

While you are putting your list together, draw or sketch your idea or invention in pencil on a separate piece of paper. This will help you think of the logic and the steps you need to take to build it. Then try to draw the invention to *scale*, with all the associated parts proportional in size to each other. A good sketch should have plenty of erase marks—so should the project-planning sheet. The more erase marks, the better, because this shows that you're thinking! Putting a working concept on paper is how inventions start.

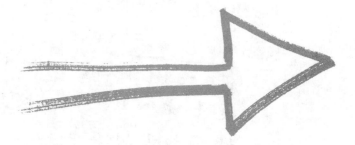

You, as a young inventor, have the luxury of getting second opinions from people like your parents. Bounce your idea off them to see what they think. If they like it, your next move may be to ask them to finance your project. (Of course, if you bring them on as investors, you have to share the rewards later. That's the rule!)

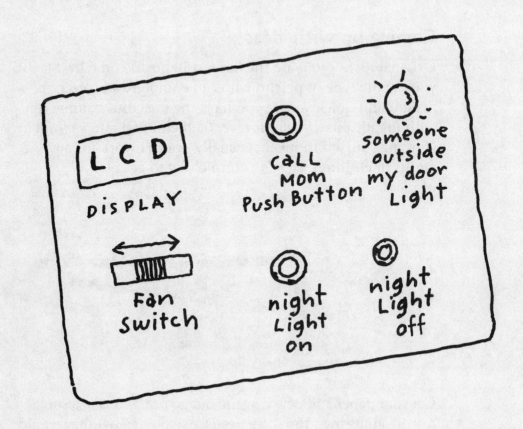

## Coming up with ideas

Original ideas often are the hardest items to come by. Maybe you are the type of person who can complete a project or assignment quickly once you have the idea, but coming up with the idea itself takes forever. Remember *pressure creativity* (forcing yourself to invent) usually doesn't work for anyone, adults or children. Here's a simple way to get plenty of ideas.

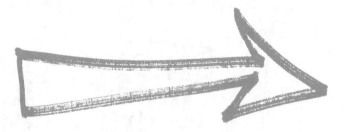

Get your paper and pencil again and go out and take a survey. Ask 10 adults their top three needs. Ask them what they would like to see in the way of an invention. Then do the same with 10 of your friends.

# Friends

1 Name        a. Need or invention # 1
                  b. Need or invention # 2
                  c. Need or invention # 3

2 Name        a.
                  b.
                  c.

3 Name        a.
                  b.
                  c.

4

5

6

7

8

9

10

# Turn on the Lights—From Bed!

*Hint:* If you can be specific in your questions and ask them in a simple-answer format, you might get better results. For example, instead of asking, "What would you invent to help the world?" you might ask two or three related questions to get your answer.

1 Old automobile tires are bad for the environment, right?

2 What practical uses can you think of for old tires?

3 Can you think of any better uses for old tires?

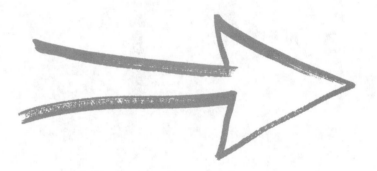

Let your parents and friends create for you! After the actual survey, tabulate your answers. If there is a similar frequent answer, there is a possibility that the majority of the population wants it! Regardless, you have just gotten yourself sixty or so ideas.

# Yes/No Survey Form (sample)

## Question #1
old Automobile tires are bad for the environment, right?

| Name | Yes | No |
|---|---|---|
| 1 Bill Smith | X | |
| 2 John Jones | X | |
| 3 | | |
| 4 | | |
| 5 | | |
| 6 | | |
| 7 | | |
| 8 | | |
| 9 | | |
| 10 | | |
| Totals | | |

## Question #2
What practical uses are there for old tires?

| Name | Answers |
|---|---|

## Young inventors become old inventors

Your inquisitive nature at an early age will most likely propel you into a technical field later in your adult life. You may find yourself going into engineering, medicine, repair or service of products, or leading-edge technologies (computers, electronics, etc.). Your interests and schooling will dictate where you start, but they might not predict where you'll end up. Doctors have invented machines and devices to help people, and attorneys have invented safer playground toys. Remember if there's a need and you can fill it, you are inventing!

Above all, by taking on projects that stir your creative juices, you have set a good precedent for your future. Technical people will always be in demand in our society. Engineering types include draftpersons, CAD operators, specification writers, sales engineers, application engineers, designers, project managers, computer programmers, and so on. The bottom line is that technical people have to know about many related topics. They have to understand electricity, machines, physics, science, chemicals, and other disciplines. Learning early how things work will help you later in life—guaranteed! So start asking yourself these questions about every thing you encounter:

☞ What's the problem?

✤ How can I solve it?

✳ What do I need?

✸ How do I do it?

✩ When can I get started?

The answers to those questions are up to you to find...except for that last one. You can get started right now!

# How to use this book

*Turn on the lights—from bed!* focuses on making useful and fun projects that solve problems and that really work. Your project or invention won't be available in any store, so you'll have the only one like it in the world—especially if you customize it with unique parts that only you might have!

But more importantly, this book teaches you how to think like an inventor. Once you can do that, you can invent all kinds of gadgets to make your life easier and more fun. And with a little inspiration, you might be able to make someone else's life easier one day. Who knows? Maybe the invention you make will be the next hot product marketed throughout the world.

## The bedroom control panel

Here's a chance to practice some scientific thinking. If you could control anything in your bedroom from the comfort of your bed—and just for fun, let's say money was no object—what would you do first? This question should get you thinking, and that thinking should produce some real needs (or at least real wants) that you can go about solving with electricity and controls. Where there's a need, there's reason to invent. Believe it or not, automating your bedroom with available technology is inventing. You don't have to develop another mousetrap or a new lightbulb to prove you are officially inventing.

Start by drawing a floor plan of your bedroom as shown. Then think about what you would like to "wire."

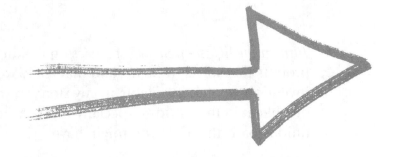

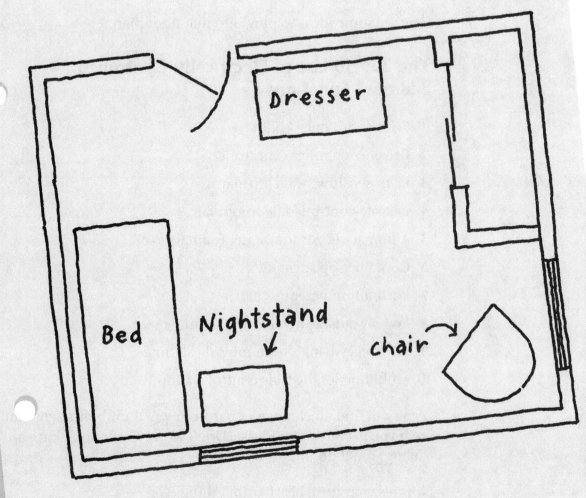

Dresser

Bed

Nightstand

chair

Bedroom floor plan

# Turn on the Lights–From Bed!

Here are some ideas to plug into that floor plan.

## The Top 10 List of Electrically Controlled Bedroom Functions

1 "The door's open" light

2 Bedside night-light controller

3 Light-sensitive, wake-up alarm

4 Remote-controlled bedroom fan

5 Automated bedroom water fountain

6 Cool fiber-optic candles!

7 Pushbutton parent signaller

8 "Who's outside my door?!" alarm

9 "The piggy bank's been moved" alarm

10 Multifunction bedside control station

If you can find an electronics parts catalog, thumb through it and see if you get any other ideas. (Don't worry if you don't have a catalog. You'll do fine without it!)

Now it's your turn. List 10 other things you could or want to automate, wire, or control. Use the sample bedroom automation list as your guide, and let your imagination run wild.

| Bedroom Automation List | | |
|---|---|---|
| No. | Description | Materials Needed |
| | | |
| | | |
| | | |
| | | |
| | | |
| | | |
| | | |
| | | |
| | | |
| | | |

# Turn on the Lights—From Bed!

## The next step

The three "C"s will help you remember to Consider Combining Concepts, or mix and match concepts for your convenience. Principles such as magnetism, motion control, temperature control, gravity, sound, light, and so on will allow you to create freely, especially if you don't limit yourself to using one at a time. Don't get discouraged if your idea won't work the way you thought it would; maybe there's another, more practical solution. If a magnetic solution won't work, try gravity. And if gravity doesn't work, try something else. Part of being a scientist, after all, is experimentation.

The flip side of this is that if you achieve success, then *take the next step!* Throughout this book, you'll have the opportunity to start with a basic idea and build on it—either by adding more parts, changing the wiring or switching, or just putting some kind of twist on it. The three Cs come in handy here, too.

For more ideas, take common electrical assemblies and take them apart. You might be able to use pieces of one assembly with pieces of another. For example, old smoke detectors should be replaced. Convince your parents that you get the old one when they get a new one. Then use the detector's horn and switch and connect it to your bedroom window as an alarm or come up with some other use for it.

When you get lots of ideas all at once, write them all down. Then try to figure out which one makes the most sense and why. Does one project cost more than another? Are some components going to be tough to find? Is one way just more fun? Use the sample provided to get an idea of how to rate and rank your brainstorms.

| item | Description of control | time + effort 1 - easy 5 hardest | $ | concept used | other reason | Final Rank 1-10 |
|---|---|---|---|---|---|---|
| A | | | | | | |
| B | | | | | | |
| C | | | | | | |
| D | | | | | | |

If you go crazy and fully wire your bedroom, remember to keep it safe. Your contraptions should be for convenience, comfort, and security. No one should get hurt. And always remember that electricity can hurt you if you don't respect and understand it. Also, you might want to let your parents in on how some of your gadgets work and where they're located (just in case you're not home one day and your super-secret "my diary's been touched" alarm won't stop beeping!).

Finally, while controlling things from your bed is an interesting and challenging concept, don't get lazy! You need to lift more than a finger for most challenges in life. Keep improving on your ideas. If you don't, somebody else might beat you to it!

There is really no cap to the bottle of electronic control schemes.

So read on, future Marie Curie, Christine Mann Darden, Thomas Edison, Benjamin Franklin, John Slaughter, or George Westinghouse. Oh, by the way, those are all famous scientists who started out as ordinary people who asked questions, thought of solutions, and made pretty cool contributions to the world of science and to our everyday lives. Are you the next?

# Now, let your parents read this

This book can give you some excellent, creative, one-on-one time with your child. Even if you don't have a technical bent, you can help your kids with these projects because the directions are clear and straightforward, with explanations to help you understand the science and technology. Even children with short attention spans can be encouraged to make these projects—as long as they are given the opportunity to contribute.

*Your* contribution is important, too. All of these projects involve electricity, and some call for using utility knives, electric drills, or hot-glue guns, so your supervision will be necessary. But you'll also contribute by brainstorming project variations with your child. The purpose of this book is to spur creative thinking in science and technology. Encourage your child to improvise. He or she may create the invention the world's been waiting for, and you'll have a great time trying together.

Perhaps most importantly, fight the temptation to skip ahead to projects toward the end of the book. The inventions presented here are arranged in a certain order, with concepts learned in one project built upon in later ones. Your child will get more out of the projects if you don't have to skip back and forth to figure out basic concepts before you take the next step.

 ## The contest

One of the best things about this book is that it makes you think. Actually, even better is that you can get paid for thinking. Honest!

All of the projects in this book are interesting and they work. But you can make them even better by trying your own variations. If you think of something really good, you can enter the **Learning Triangle Press SciTech Invention** competition. You might even win first prize—$500 in cash! See the back of this book for your contest entry form.

And get ready to use your brain!

## Symbols

The following symbols are used in the book:

### Adult supervision

Requires adult supervision

### The next step

How to alter a project, build on a concept, or put a spin on the previous idea

### Cool ideas!

Ideas for going further. Also, potential inventions for the Learning Triangle Press SciTech Invention Contest

### History/fun fact

Historical or other background info of projects

### Scientific terms

Important terms being defined; can also be found in the glossary

# Project 1

# Wired vs. wireless

# Project 1

**A**RE YOU AFRAID OF ELECTRICITY? I'M NOT TALKING about thunderstorms and lightning—they'll scare the best of us. Rather, are you a little scared of electrically wiring things? It's certainly not a bad idea to have respect for the powerful thing electricity is. But there is no electrical voltage that can hurt you if the power source has first been disconnected. The best thing you can do to conquer your fear is to learn about electricity. It can't hurt you if you understand it.

Electricity powers many of the appliances and things we use. From the wall outlet in your bedroom to the speaker in your radio-alarm clock, wires and cable are bringing electrons to their destination. You might not know it, but the power at your bedroom wall receptacle is brought there through wires that come into your house from somewhere outside (either from the telephone pole or from underground). All that power originates at a power-generating station, where the power is generated by either coal, oil, or nuclear power. Big wires carry power from the station to your home. Then the wires get smaller and smaller. If you've ever seen an appliance that's been taken apart, you've probably seen all the different sizes and colors of wires inside. Once the power has entered an appliance, the wire has gotten very small!

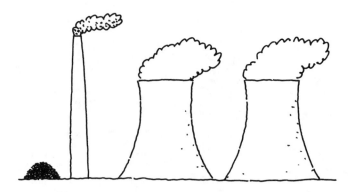

As a young inventor, you're going to be concerned with small wires. Big wires usually carry larger amounts of electricity—amounts that can be very dangerous to humans who don't respect it. When used properly, electricity can be a tremendous tool. Remember, you must always treat electricity with the utmost respect. You can't see it, you usually can't hear it, and you won't smell it unless some electrical component is already overloaded and burning!

 ## Science stuff

Once electricity enters an appliance, it has to be dispersed throughout to all the powered components. Sometimes, the electricity goes through a *transformer*. A transformer is a device made of many metallic plates and coils of wire around those plates that allows electricity at a higher voltage to be "stepped-down" to a lower value inside the appliance. (This is why the wire size can be smaller inside an appliance.) Sometimes, the metallic plates vibrate as the electricity passes through them, and this makes a noise.

# Project 1

*Electricity* is the flow of negatively charged electrons from one point to another. Electrons travel through a *conductor* (any material that allows for the flow, or conduction, of electrons). Metal is a conductor, and the metallic inner material of a wire allows the electrons to flow to their source. As you can see (see the top illustration on this page), wire usually has an outer casing made of a nonconductive plastic, often called the *insulator*. Most wire used today is either aluminum or copper—softer metals that bend. The amount of aluminum or copper within a given plastic casing is called the *wire gauge*, or *diameter*. (See the bottom illustration on this page.)

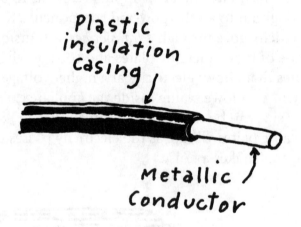

Plastic insulation casing

Metallic Conductor

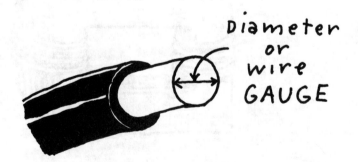

Diameter or wire GAUGE

Now pay attention because this part can be a bit confusing. The wire gauge is a number assigned to a certain thickness, cross-section, or diameter of a piece of wire. As the wire gauge number increases, the actual diameter decreases (see the table below). For the projects in this book, you will be working mainly with smaller wires, which carry low voltages and low currents. But you'll be amazed what you can do with a little bit of wire!

### Common wire gauges and sizes

| Wire Gauge | Diameter* | Comment |
|---|---|---|
| 24 | 0.0201 | Used as control wiring |
| 22 | 0.0253 | " " |
| 20 | 0.0320 | " " |
| 18 | 0.0403 | " " |
| 16 | 0.0508 | |
| 14 | 0.0641 | Residential 115-vac wiring |
| 12 | 0.0808 | " " |
| 10 | 0.1019 | |
| 8 | 0.1285 | more than ⅛" diameter |

*Inches–not including the wire's plastic casing.

First, a few basic things to remember about the properties of wire (many are illustrated on page 6).

1   When using wire, you want to make it easy for the electrons to flow from point to point. *Resistance* is the property within a wire that slows down the flow of electrons—they start bumping into each other and into other atoms. This resistance shows up initially as heat, which makes the wire warm. The perfect control wiring scheme will not have any warm wires.

2   Long wire runs have greater resistance, so they can get warm quicker than short runs of the same gauge wire. Keep this in mind as you plan your projects.

3   Thin wires sometimes present a problem because they limit the room the electrons have to travel in. The potential for bumping into other atoms is greater when the "highway" is small and crowded. Thick wires, on the other hand, give the electrons plenty of room—and plenty of passing lanes!

4   Thick, short wire runs are the best.

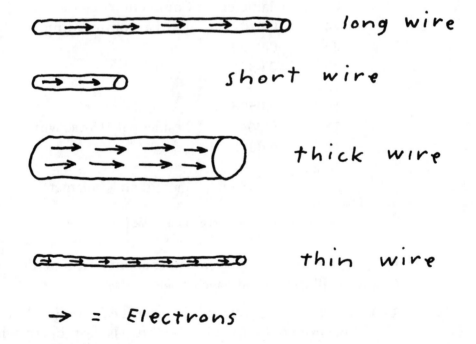

Using wire to start, stop, and power electrical things is called *control*. Throughout this book, you will be challenged to control multiple electrical components in a way that puts you in the driver's seat. You will have control because you can make the control package yourself!

Introducing switches and other electrical components at strategic locations in an *electrical circuit,* the roadmap of wiring, makes you a control engineer. Today's control engineers use available electrical devices and *assemblies* whenever they're available. They don't reinvent the basics. Assembled and packaged electrical components make building control systems easier.

There will be times when you want to control the operation of a device in a very exact way. For example, you might want a light to go "on" instead of "off" whenever the switch is thrown. This involves *normally open (n.o.)* and *normally closed (n.c.)* circuits and switches. We'll cover this topic more completely later in this book, but, for now, just remember that electricity flows when contacts are closed in a switch, and it doesn't flow when they're open.

## Wireless

In wire-based electrical circuits, electricty flows at some voltage and current level. You control the voltage and current by starting and stopping the flow of electricity, usually with switches. Anything you want to control, either remotely or locally, can be controlled with wires. However, these days, the main method of control is with *wireless* devices, or remote control.

Wireless control actually uses high-frequency radio waves, sent through the air, to start and stop the flow of electricity (ironically at a wired part) within another device. The frequency is the number of times every cycle a pulse in that radio wave strikes the receiver. For comparison, your ac electricity travels over wires through your house at 60 cycles per second. That's a lot, but wireless remote controls are usually pulsing at much higher rates. (See the frequency table on page 8.)

# Project 1

## Various frequency bands

| Acronym | Range | Use |
| --- | --- | --- |
| **VLF**<br>Very Low Frequency | 2-30 kHz | timing signals<br>industrial controllers |
| **LF**<br>Low Frequency | 30-300 kHz | navigational |
| **MF**<br>Medium Frequency | 300-3000 kHz | land, sea mobile |
| **HF**<br>High Frequency | 3-30 MHz | aircraft mobile |
| **VHF**<br>Very High Frequency | 30-300 MHz | radio and TV<br>broadcasting |
| **UHF**<br>Ultra High Frequency | 300-3000 MHz | space and satellite<br>communication |
| **SHF**<br>Super High Frequency | 3-30 GHz | space and satellite<br>communication |

*Notes:*
1. The High Frequency (HF) range is also called "shortwave."
2. Audible frequencies are 30 Hz to 18 kHz (for younger people) and 100 Hz to 10 kHz (for older people).
3. The radio-frequency wave that "carries" information is called the carrier wave.
4. kHz = kilohertz; MHz = megahertz; GHz = gigahertz.

Wireless devices actually require two components, a transmitter and receiver. The transmitter is often battery-powered, and it converts that dc energy into high-frequency radio waves. These radio waves can be directed to a device that contains a radio-wave receiver, which will decode the signal. A start, or "on," signal from the transmitter will have its own particular frequency, while the stop, or "off," signal will be at another frequency. These different frequencies allow for multiple functions in a wireless controller.

Your television's wireless remote control device has many functions built into it. It can start and stop both the TV and the VCR along with muting, channel, volume, and other control. Each of these functions requires a different frequency be transmitted, which then has to be properly decoded at the receiving device to provide the right result. If you have ever taken a remote control device apart (or had one fall apart), you can see that it is a static device with no moving parts. Its main components are the battery, board, and *oscillator*, which develops the desired frequencies.

## You are in control

Whether you choose to use wires or wireless control, you can "automate" things all around you!  All you have to do is dream up the desire and link components together. Once at this point, think of the ways to bring electricity to and from some of the components. Ask yourself many questions. How can you improve or increase an activity? What should be turned on and off, and why? If no power or electricity is used by a device now, what could you make happen if you introduced some?

Another place for great ideas for things you can control is electronics magazines. These magazines—especially the ones put out by electronic parts stores and novelty shops—actually provide ideas with the components they carry. For example, you might notice a certain type of switch in these catalogs that makes you think of another device you want to control. You have just had an idea *and* solution at the same time!

You can often come up with ideas for controls by visiting stores that carry high-tech products. Often, when new "high-tech" products are introduced, they're very expensive. Consider their premise and how they are built. What controls them? Take the concept home with you, and try to duplicate it. You just might surprise yourself.

## Scrounging for basic parts

Have you ever considered how many appliances are thrown away every day? Probably thousands, and the sad fact is that about 90 percent of their parts are reusable. Remember, good inventors are resourceful. Get the switches, wire, and other electrical "goodies" from old, discarded appliances, computers, games, toys, and anything electronic. Save them. You'll minimize the amount of your own money you'll have to spend on parts, and you might even find an assembly or device that will either be the "missing link" to one of your puzzles or will give you a completely new idea.

No matter what you do with them, salvaging wire and parts from discarded appliances and toys will teach you good "un-wiring" techniques. After all, it takes as much work and skill to disconnect electrical components as it does to connect them properly. You will find, as you progress in the electrical field, that wiring is a skill and it takes practice to be good at it.

## To wire or not to wire?

Wired or wireless? Which is better? The answer is...it depends! A wireless package will initially cost more than a wired package, but it provides much greater flexibility. It can be moved around and has a better range than the wired package. A wired remote control has a range limited to the length of wire attached. That wire also gets tangled easily.

Which is better for your application? You ask the questions, and you answer them. If the pluses outweigh the minuses, you've made your decision. Every situation has its best solution.

# Something you can try

To illustrate how sound waves can travel over a wire—or, in this case, a string—let's simulate the first telephone call. The sound waves travel through the string much like electrical waves travel through wire. You could perform this same project with wire and achieve similar results. A perfect application for this can-to-can network could be from your treehouse to the house. Then maybe your parents wouldn't have to yell for you to come to dinner! Oh, and speaking of parents, be sure to have an adult help you with the drilling.

## Stuff you'll need

☞ 2 small tin cans (cleaned and rinsed, or you'll get tomato soup on your ear!)

❀ 40-50 feet of string

✳ Drill

## How to do it

1  Drill a small hole into the center of each can's bottom. Make sure that the hole is relatively smooth and free of jagged edges. We don't want anybody getting cut during this project!

2  Tie a large knot at one end of the string. Make sure it is bigger than the smaller hole you previously drilled into the tin can's bottom.

# Project 1

**3**  Thread the string through the first can and into the second can. Tie a similar knot at the other end of the string.

**4**  Now stretch the string between the two cans so that the line of string is stretched tightly. When you speak into your can, the person listening at the other can will be able to hear every word you say.

*Famous names in electricity*  Many of the early pioneers in electricity are recognized for their major contributions to particular technologies. Following is a list of some of those key individuals, their claim to fame, when they lived, where they were from, and a fun fact or two regarding each. You no doubt will recognize many of the names. Maybe someday your own name will appear on a list like this one!

**Alexander Graham Bell** lived from 1847 until 1922. He was born in Scotland and later came to the United States. He is credited with inventing the telephone, but he was also instrumental in helping the deaf and those with speech problems.

**Thomas Alva Edison** was a United States inventor who lived from 1847 to 1931. He is credited with nearly 1,000 inventions. Among them were the incandescent electric lamp, the motion-picture projector, the phonograph, and the very first industrial research laboratory. He is linked strongly to the General Electric Company and was an advocate of dc electricity. (He lost his cause...see Westinghouse, below.)

**Michael Faraday** was a physicist from Great Britain. He was born in 1791 and died in 1867. He is regarded as the father of electromagnetism. His Law of Induction is still taught in schools and colleges all over the world. This law is the basis for electric motors. Michael Faraday was originally a bookseller and eventually wrote several books.

**Benjamin Franklin** was a United States scientist, writer, and statesman. He was born in 1706 and died in 1790. He was also amazing! He invented bifocals, the Franklin stove, and the lightning rod (remember him and that kite?). He was even a printer and publisher. But perhaps his best abilities were his negotiating skills between the U.S. and England.

**Guglielmo Marconi** was an Italian scientis who lived from 1874 to 1937. He is credited with discovering the wireless telegraph. If he could only see those couch potatoes flipping through the cable stations with their remote controls today!

**Nikola Tesla** was born in 1856 in Croatia and died in New York in 1943. His inventions included the rotating magnetic field (the principle used in most electric motors today) and transformers. He could simulate manmade lightning, and he developed the famous Tesla coil, which was eventually used in many televisions and radios.

**George Westinghouse** lived most of his life in New York. He was born in 1846 and died in 1914. His main invention was the air brake and, combined with his other electrical inventions, he was instrumental in the railroad industry, especially with signaling. Later, he promoted the adoption of ac electricity throughout the country against a lot of opposition. He persisted, and eventually ac power prevailed.

# No knock...
# who's there?

Unless you are an only child (and maybe even then), you probably sometimes have trouble getting a little privacy. It's really a pain when you have friends over and you're right in the middle of a secret conversation . . . only to find out your creep of a brother is lurking outside your bedroom door and has heard every word. Now every kid in school will know that you've got a crush on the kid down the street! What a brat!

## Problem?

You have invited your best friend over for a weekend sleepover, and you want to be alone to trade secrets and hang art in your room. However, your annoying little brother is trying to "spy" on you. He thinks he's being sneaky, but you want to find a way to catch him red-handed!

## Solution?

Create a device that will alert you and your friend that your snoopy sibling is just outside your closed bedroom door. By utilizing cool, electronic technology you can catch him and get him sent to *his* room for quite awhile!

First, don't tell your sibling that you are going to do anything. A good magician never reveals his or her secret and neither should you, the inventor. Next, get your friend to help. You both will learn, have fun while doing it, and get that private time you deserve away from your annoying brother. (Of course, this project works just as well for the boys and their bothersome sisters). Once you've told your friend of the idea, start thinking about when you'll get the hardware you need, where you'll mount it, and how you'll alert your parents once you've caught the culprit!

## Science stuff

You could use any number of different scientific and electrical principles to catch your tormenter. There are motion sensors that can detect body heat and any type of motion. You could also use complex light transmitters and receivers that will trigger an alarm when the beam of light is broken. On the other hand, both of these are more complicated and expensive than you really need. You need a simple way of knowing that someone is trying to look through the keyhole in your bedroom door.

"Geeky brother"

Motion Lights

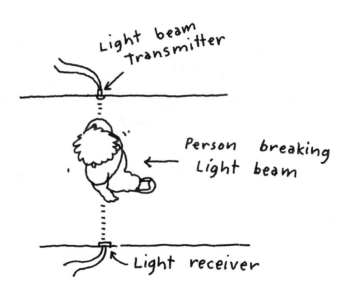

Light beam transmitter

Person breaking Light beam

Light receiver

# Project 2

The **switch** is the key element in your trap, and you have many to choose from. The best choice for this project is a foot switch—a vibration-sensitive switch that, when bumped by your brother, completes the electrical circuit and signals you. We will select the foot switch. When placed appropriately in the right spot under a floor mat outside of your bedroom door, any person's weight will trigger the switch, light the signal light in your room, and he's caught!

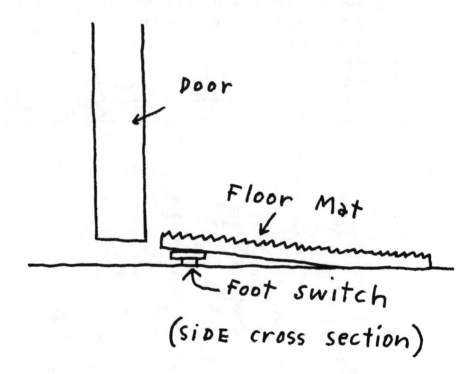

Door

Floor Mat

Foot switch

(SIDE cross section)

## Stuff you'll need

☐ 1 foot switch (Radio Shack #44-610 or equivalent)

☐ 1 9-volt dc battery

☐ 1 battery holder

- ☐ 1 floor carpet mat with solid, hard backing
- ☐ some wire
- ☐ wire cutters
- ☐ electrical tape
- ☐ 1 9-volt flashlight bulb or equivalent (match your power source)
- ☐ 1 bulb holder

## How to do it

1 Following the illustration (or your own floor plan), decide where you will mount the light in your room.

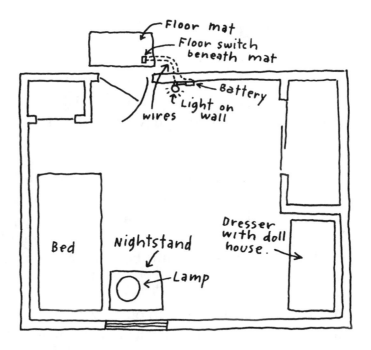

2  Next, mount the light, battery holder, and bulb holder.

3  Before you cut any length of wire, prepare the foot switch. You might have to cut one end to accommodate the wires coming from the battery/light.

4  Once you have prepared the foot switch, cut a suitable length of wire, allowing yourself some extra in case you need to move the switch or light to another location.

5  Cover the foot switch with the floor mat, centering the mat over the switch and positioning the whole assembly where you predict your culprit will stand first. Remember to try and hide the switch and wires as best you can.

6  Insert the battery and test the device. If it works to your liking, close your door and wait for the "spy!"

 ## Cool ideas

You can vary this project any way you want. You can even set it up to work at night when you are asleep. In this case, you might want a sound-based alarm instead of a light. Maybe a little chime alarm or beeper that goes off whenever someone steps on your floor mat!

One logical extension to the project is to add an "Alert-Mom-that-little-brother-is-annoying-me" signal to the project. Once you've caught him outside of your door, you can push another button that signals your parent in another room. When you think about it, there's nothing better than completely automating the whole procedure!

You also can experiment with other switches and other sensors. You might even want to run a length of wire into the bathroom.

Why? So that you will know when the bathroom is available, of course! A light in your bedroom can go "on" when the bathroom light is "off."

## The next step

Would you like to have some real fun with this project? Instead of simply detecting the presence of someone outside of your bedroom door, how about catching them on camera? You will have to have access to a video camera—not an inexpensive item to use in a project, but these days very common in many households. If your family has a video camera they'll let you use, you're set.

You will need a longer cable (available at Radio Shack, etc.) to reach into a TV in your bedroom if you want to watch in "real time." If you can't watch the culprit "live," then make sure the video camera's battery is fully charged, and load a tape. This project will sharpen your electrical control skills as well as making a pretty good secret agent out of you!

A critical phase of this project and the one element that will make it a success will be your ability to conceal the camera so you can catch the intruder without him or her even knowing. To accomplish this we will need a *blind*. A blind is a camouflaged housing that will hide the camera in the hallway.

You will need a cardboard box into which you will hide the camera. It doesn't have to be much bigger than the video camera itself (remember, you're trying to be as inconspicuous as possible). As shown (see illustration on the next page), cut a hole into one end of the box. Next, run a power extension cord to the camera along with the extended video cable. Make sure you have

# Project 2

concealed them as well as possible. Cover the box with some dirty clothes (make it look like a pile ready for the washing machine), and also cover any cables or wires. Put a tape into the video recorder and hit "play." If you have a TV screen set up in your bedroom and you are fully connected, sit back and wait for the action!

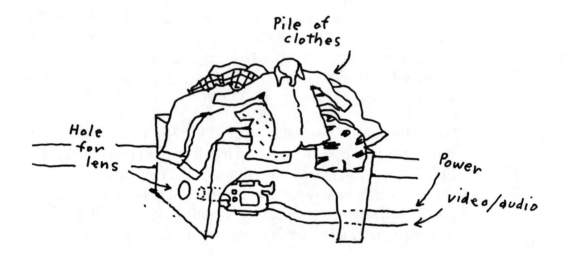

Pile of clothes

Hole for lens

Power

video/audio

# Project **3**

# Everybody's a comedian

**D**ID YOU EVER NOTICE THAT WHEN ONE OF A GROUP OF people starts to laugh, it's almost impossible for everyone else not to join in? There's something about the sound of laughter that's . . . well, funny. But did you ever tell a great joke and no one laughed? Maybe they weren't paying attention, or maybe they didn't get it, but you *know* it was a great joke, and if just one person would've laughed, everyone else would be rolling on the floor with tears streaming down their faces. Maybe you just need a little help with your act.

## Problem?

You, the future stand-up comedian, are practicing jokes on your family. How do you make sure that you get the laughs you deserve?

## Solution?

Since you are a one-person show, you're going to have to arrange for your own laughs. The professionals have support people helping them. Have you ever noticed the "laugh" or "applause" signs and lights that control audiences? (These signs also explain why you hear people laughing on TV when something's not even funny!) Well, we'll assume that you don't have *that* luxury, but you can get laughs the same way that professionals do—with taped or "canned" laughter. How are you going to do that? With your pocket remote controller, of course!

# Science stuff

You could build your own wireless transmitter and receiver to use as your laugh track. This would involve assembling some *integrated circuits* (ICs), *light-emitting diodes* (LEDs), transistors, capacitors, resistors, and some batteries on a couple of breadboards. A battery-powered signal is generated and transmitted via one of the LEDs. That signal is then transmitted as a sign pattern to the receiver LED, where it is decoded and the appropriate activity is commanded.

Obviously, it is much simpler just to purchase the ready-to-go, already-packaged remote control transmitter and receiver, and our project will proceed on that basis. To get those laughs when the audience doesn't think you're funny, all you need are a few items.

## Stuff you'll need

- [ ] 1 cassette tape recorder
- [ ] 1 wireless remote transmitter
  (Radio Shack #61-2667, or equivalent)
- [ ] 1 wireless receiver (Radio Shack #61-2667, or equivalent)
- [ ] an electrical outlet
- [ ] some masking tape
- [ ] some good (or bad) jokes

## How to do it

1   First, practice your own laugh—you know, the good one! Then get a couple of your friends together for a "laugh

session." Spend some time cracking each other up and record your best laughs. Make a 10- to 15-minute recording of just you and your friends laughing as hard as you can.

2   Next, check out the room where you plan to hold your major presentation. Look for an inconspicuous outlet. Place the remote receiver in that outlet and plug in the tape recorder.

Have the tape player already in the "play" switch position, rewound, with the volume up!

3   Tape the remote control receiver to your hand, arm, or wrist. Try to keep in concealed.

4   Gather your family later that evening, and start telling your best (or worst) jokes. When they don't laugh, touch the "on" button on your remote control transmitter (hidden in your pocket). Once they hear your canned laughter, they won't be able to help themselves, even if your joke is bad. The sound of laughter always gets 'em—guaranteed!

5   Get some *good* jokes—it'll be no time at all until the tape runs out.

## Tips

☞ When you are recording your canned laughter, try to keep the entire recording as close to constant, upbeat laughter. Don't allow any distracting background noise or talking to be recorded.

❃ To completely hide the remote control transmitter, wear a long-sleeved shirt. Tape the transmitter on your arm, higher up than your wrist and under the shirt sleeve. When you're delivering your punch lines, have your arms crossed. You'll easily be able to press the "on" button to summon the laughs, on command, and not be detected. Of course, you'll have to remember the positions of the "on" and "off" pushbuttons under your sleeve.

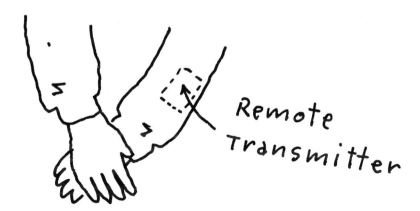

Remote Transmitter

 **Cool ideas**

You could explore the remote-control idea further by using motion sensors and detectors. If you have money to burn, you could check into light-beam sensor systems. Actually, these systems use infrared photoelectrics and relays. These cool ideas are more expensive to try, but they'll give you a good look at leading-edge technology. Some of these principles will be used somewhere in your future life. Best to get an understanding of them now!

Have you ever lost a remote control? Sometimes tricky to find, huh? With all the VCRs, TVs, CD players, and so on controlled remotely, pretty soon there will be too many individual remote controls in your home. What should you do about this? A wristwatch that'll house all the various miniature remotes? How about a remote controller built into your computer or computer workstation? Or is there a better way altogether? This might be your chance to head off a future social dilemma! Remember, where there is a need, there will be an invention!

## The next step

Just as you got the laughs that you deserved for your stand-up comedy routine, you also can get some "oohs and ahs" along with some applause for doing some magic tricks.

What could you have ready to run via a remote controller that would amaze your friends? A fan or pump maybe? Moving a little air or water on command always gets 'em. How about a levitation trick? Could you have a small dc motor ready to pull a sheet into the air? All you need is a motor connected to a low-voltage power supply (changes ac power to dc) plugged into the wall outlet. The possibilities are only limited to your imagination!

Following the same procedures with the remote control transmitter and plug-in receiver, let's perform a levitation trick. Follow the illustration, and try to do this trick after dinner when the lights are turned down low. You might even want to do the trick in the basement or garage (with even less light). Low levels of light will help to conceal threads or wire for your act (after all, the big-time magicians use low lights and dark stages, too).

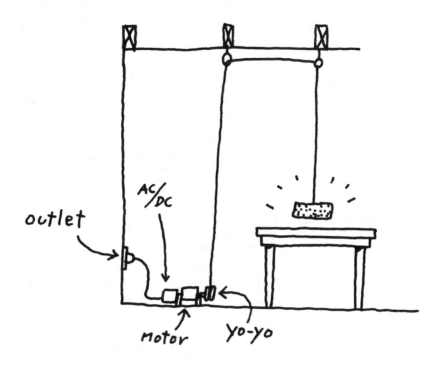

In addition to the remote-control items you used for your laugh track, you will need:

- [ ] some thread or fishing line (a dark color, about 30 feet of it)
- [ ] 1 sponge
- [ ] 1 napkin
- [ ] a small table
- [ ] 1 dc motor with plug-in power supply
- [ ] 2 pulleys (one for on the motor and one to put above you at the ceiling)

# Project 3

*Is it magic?* Technology is playing a much larger role in the world of magic—sometimes not to entertain but to deceive. Whenever you are being entertained, ask yourself how the trick is being done. Some gadget or device is being employed; just look. Some magicians have another person "at the controls," pushing buttons to make things move at the precise time, in sync with the magician. Many so-called mind readers trick the audience by using a very small wireless receiver, which they have near their ear. Another person reads cards that the audience filled out beforehand (which also locate them within the audience). The second person then transmits a voice message to the "mind reader's" receiver. The personal things written down earlier by a person in a particular seat seem to be things that the mind reader is "picking-up!"

## How to do it

1  Before dinner, set all items up in the basement (or wherever your presentation will take place). Follow the illustration, but select the best location for each item in the trick to suit your basement or garage. Make sure you conceal all items well.

2  *Plug* in the remote receiver. Plug the power supply into the motor, and connect the motor to the power supply.

3  Next, connect a pulley (even a small yo-yo will work) to the motor shaft (get the rotation correct), and route the thread or thin wire up over another pulley or even a smooth nail down to your sponge.

4  Attach the thread to the sponge on the table, cover the sponge with a napkin, and practice your trick a couple of times. Your sleight of hand will also play a key role in the success of this trick! When you say the magic words, the sponge will begin to rise. It rises because you previously taped the remote control transmitter to your arm, under your shirt, and quickly hit the "on" button as you said the magic words.

5  Unless you're ambitious enough to figure out a way to bring the sponge and napkin back down (by rigging up the motor), you'll have to end your trick by grabbing the napkin and sponge out of the air. It will slide right off of the nail assembly and, if all goes well, your audience will be left wondering how you did it!

# Project 4

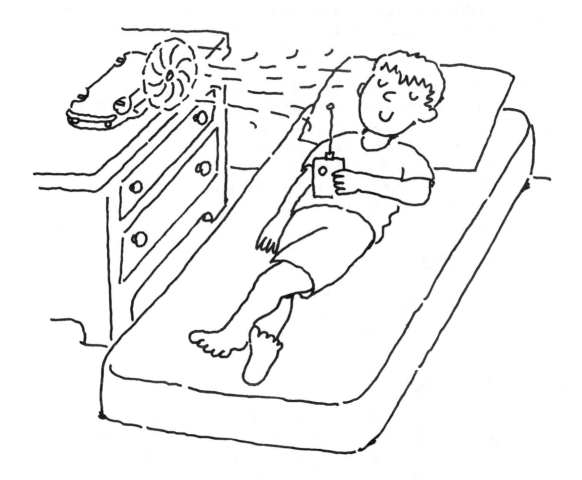

# Cool wheels

**D**OES YOUR BEDROOM EVER GET STUFFY IN THE MIDDLE of the night? You could get up and turn on a fan, of course, but then comes the dilemma of turning off the fan when you've cooled off and you're starting to drift off to sleep. By the time you get up and turn off the fan, you're wide awake again. Hmmmm, how would a genius inventor solve this problem?

Well, in this case, let's think of another problem. How many remote-control toys do you have lying around the house? Robots, cars, little motorcycles, airplanes, and so on. Chances are, you've either lost interest in them or they're starting to show the years of wear. Or maybe your friends don't think it's "cool" to play with these types of toys anymore. What can you do with this excess of unwanted remote-control items?

## Problem?

Is there a way to solve the problem of the stuffy bedroom at the same time you solve the problem of the uncool, worn-out remote-control toys?

## Solution?

No, you don't need to sell the toys at a garage sale where you also pick up a cheap fan! Instead, impress your friends with your creativity and resourcefulness with a remote-control fan made out of an old toy. Using the basic components of that neglected toy—the radio transmitter, the receiver, the power pack, and the motor—you can create a practical and oh-so-cool remote-control fan.

The better news with this project is that we will not have to invest a lot of money in getting something practical out of it. This project actually will be a little more labor-intensive because you'll have to work at changing the physical parts of your old toy. Since you probably will also make permanent changes to it, you should decide first that you really don't want that old toy car to be a car anymore.

# Science stuff

A remote-controlled car is actually a radio-controlled device. Radio waves are generated by the transmitter, sent through the air, and received by the receiver. Once received, a decoder interprets the signals as "go slower" or "go faster" (Some cars can run 1,350 feet per minute, which is equivalent to 15 miles per hour! That's pretty fast for a little toy car!). Sometimes the signals are interpreted as "turn left" or "turn right" or "open or close" things on the car.

Receiver

Transmitter

Remote control
(Radio waves)

These radio waves are traveling at typical frequencies of 27 or 49 megahertz (MHz) through the air. The FM radios that bring us music have a range of 88 to 108 megahertz as assigned by the Federal Communications Commission (FCC). This means that the lower frequency transmissions of the toys won't interfere with the higher frequency FM music stations (see illustration on the next page).

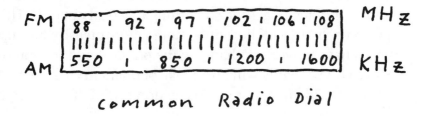

common Radio Dial

Go find that old, not-used-anymore remote-control car and its controller. To keep it simple, you should also locate a small plastic fan blade or propeller. Make sure the batteries are charged and ready to go. After this project, you will be ready to move on to the big stuff—those discarded remote-control answering machines and VCRs that mom and dad don't want anymore!

## Stuff you'll need

- ☐ remote-control car
- ☐ remote-control car transmitter
- ☐ the charged battery pack
- ☐ one 12- or 9-volt ac-to-dc power supply (optional; use if battery pack is not available)
- ☐ 1 plastic fan blade
- ☐ 1 wooden shaft, 2″ long by ½″ in diameter
- ☐ hot-glue gun
- ☐ screwdriver
- ☐ hammer (optional; use only if you have to!)
- ☐ cardboard box
- ☐ scissors or utility knife

# How to do it

1  First, take the car body housing off of the car (that is what the screwdriver is for!). You won't be needing that plastic car housing anymore (unless you *want* your fan to look like an old car!), and removing the housing will make it easier for you to mount the remaining assembly somewhere with ease.

2  Next, remove the wheels, especially the ones that are actually driven by the transmitter. This is where you will attach the fan blade.

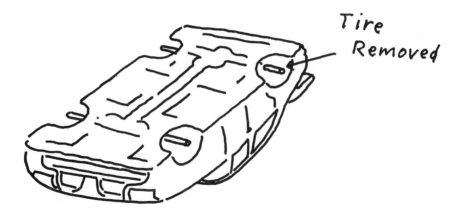

3  Cut openings in the cardboard box for the fan blade shaft to protrude through. Cover the remote car base. Decorate the box anyway if you want.

4  Secure the fan blade to the stub shaft from the motor that previously drove the wheel. You might want to use a hot glue gun for this.

5  Set the whole assembly on a counter and make sure the fan blade will turn freely with no obstructions.

6  Have a seat and turn on your auto-fan. Adjust the fan speed as you like.

7  Enjoy the cool air!

## Cool ideas

The possibilities are almost endless with your remote control car. One thing to keep in mind is that the rechargeable battery will still have to be recharged. Sorry about that . . . but you still will be able to amaze your friends with a contraption or two.

You could attach a pulley or gear to the output shaft of the car's motor and drive a multitude of other things. For instance, you could make a mini-conveyor for moving sand, dirt, or other materials. You could even make that system into a bucket conveyor.

Another good use of your discarded car would be to use it as a remote-controlled agitator or mixer. By turning the car on its side and attaching a mixing blade of some sort with hot glue, you can instantly have yourself a remote-controlled mixer. By moving the mixing blade in the forward direction and then in reverse, you have now made it an agitator. Perhaps you or your parents have a certain mixture which needs to be stirred every few minutes so that it doesn't get hard. You could be off doing something else and still keep the mix agitated from afar!

Another cool idea would be to take some wheels, a car body, a motor, a battery pack, and a remote-radio controller from many different sources and create or build your very own custom car! You might find this approach both cost-effective (cheaper than buying a top-of-the-line car in the toy store) and extremely challenging. Start thinking about it, and start gathering the parts!

Taking a remote-control car apart enough to get a useful, working product out of it can even make for an interesting science fair project. As a matter of fact, if you can disguise your project enough so that it doesn't look like a remote-control car, you just might be onto something that could win you a prize.

# The next step

How about this one: a remote-controlled scarecrow for the garden. You could turn your old race car into a noisemaker that will scare the birds and other critters from your garden. And the good news is that you don't really need to spend much time making an actual scarecrow. The scarecrow isn't what will scare the birds and critters; it's the noise you create. Of course, if you want a true, 24-hour patrol, you might want to put some time into making a truly scary scarecrow.

*Scarecrow with Pots and Pans Attached*

*Remote Car Body*

The scarecrow gets attached to the remote control car motor and turns with the rest of the noise-making parts. When you can see the "garden invaders" from your window, press a button and "shoo" them away! By attaching some noisy, clanging objects to the motor output shaft, you can get those objects to collide and bang together to make noise as the shaft turns. Foil piepans, old forks and spoons, almost any metallic part will work well to bang and clang together. Just tie them to the scarecrow so that they hang close to each other. Even an old bell or two will scare those crows away!

*Did you know...* Did you know that every radio-controlled car and product needs a power pack or battery to run? These batteries are usually rechargeable, which means that they can be inserted into a 120-volt house outlet or a 12-volt dc car battery to be charged.

A 30-minute battery means that the battery is fully charged in 30 minutes, not that it will give you 30 minutes of fun and running time after it is charged (usually, it's much less). Also, these rechargeable battery packs are typically made of Ni-Cd (Ni is the symbol for the chemical element nickel, and Cd is the symbol for the chemical element cadmium). Rechargeable batteries initially cost more than throw-away batteries, but, over a couple of years of life, they will save you energy costs over repeatedly buying disposable batteries. Also, because disposable batteries aren't good for the environment, rechargeable batteries are an earth-smart choice.

If you use a battery on a really hot day, it actually produces more energy. But if you store a battery in a very hot place, it will start to deteriorate faster. Always store batteries in cool, dry areas (40-50 degrees Fahrenheit). Batteries like to operate best in 65-70 degree Fahrenheit temperatures. At cold temperatures, you have two things working against you: one, the battery puts out less usable energy and two, it won't last long at all. Keep temperature in mind whenever you store batteries and when you run them!

By moving the joystick control to forward and reverse, you will get the scarecrow to *oscillate* back and forth. This motion will cause lots of clanging and noise! This project will make good use out of an old remote-control car (even a broken one—as long as motor and controls work!).

As time marches on, so does technology. Remote-control devices and products are everywhere: in industry, in the workplace, and in your homes. As time goes on, there will be newer and better remote-control products as older technology gives way to the new. There will be plenty of older-style, discarded remote-control components to experiment with. You can create some awesome assemblies if you set your mind to it. See what you can come up with!

# Project 5

# Who needs a cat?

THE CLICHÉ "BUILD A BETTER MOUSETRAP," IS USED over and over because, over the years, many inventors have tried to conjure up the perfect alternative to the typical spring-activated mousetrap. But you can build something to be used in conjunction with the mousetrap. The mousetrap alarm!

That mouse that's terrorizing everyone in your house is seldom seen. Mice tend to travel around your house in very inconspicuous places. They can be found in behind cupboards, in your attic or basement, in drop ceilings, and sometimes even inside your walls. These are all hard-to-get-to places. What's more, if you place a trap where a mouse might amble into it, that place is going to be hard to see from normal places in the house. Once you have crawled into one of those hard-to-get-to places to set the trap, who wants to crawl back until you are sure the little critter has been caught? This is where your handy-dandy mousetrap alarm comes into play!

## Problem?

How many mice have been caught, only to get away before you can dispose of them? If you're a mouse and you get caught in a trap, your only option is to try everything to escape, and many succeed. So how can you, the family inventor and protector from mice, find out exactly when the mouse trips the trap?

## Solution?

You can place an alarm at the trap that will go off as soon as the mouse activates it. This way, you can get to the mouse and dispose of it before it escapes. But can you go to the hardware store and purchase one of these alarms? No! You have to put your creative-controls thinking cap on, and then you can build one.

## Science stuff

What type of sensor or switch will best be suited for your scheme? There are vibration sensors, *normally open (N.O.)* alarm switches, *normally closed (NC)* alarm switches, tamper-proof switches, magnetic switches, and more. For this project, keep it simple! Use a normally open alarm switch, the first time around. They are inexpensive, reliable, and can be used with a battery powered circuit.

## Tips

Before you try to convince dad and mom that this is a good idea, make sure it is! Usually when your parents have decided to set a trap, they want to catch that mouse (which is now a pest) quickly. Your wiring scheme must be ready to go. Also, make sure that the run of wire to the alarm is not too long or troublesome to actually do. You should have all the parts ready ahead of time and know that the scheme will work. Experiment beforehand. You also need to decide if you your alarm will go "on" when the mouse is caught or go "off" when the mouse is caught. Having the alarm go "on" will use much less power, so that's probably the way to go.

OK, so the rodent has been heard running around in the attic and your family has declared war on the furry, four-legged creature. Now is the time to spring into action!

# Project 5

## Stuff you'll need

- [ ] 1 N.O. (normally open) alarm switch
- [ ] 1 mousetrap
- [ ] 1 flashlight bulb with bulb holder
- [ ] 1 battery (voltage compatible with flashlight bulb)
- [ ] 1 battery holder
- [ ] 20-25 feet of wire
- [ ] some double-sided tape
- [ ] electrical tape
- [ ] some bait (coated with peanut butter for best results) wrapped onto the trap with thread

*and* . . . 1 mouse (this may be very hard to obtain!)

## How to do it

1  Let an adult help. Your mom or dad can take care of the actual mousetrap baiting and preparation. You start wiring and mounting.

2  Follow the wiring scheme, and start by mounting the alarm light and battery somewhere visible just below the attic (or wherever you're placing your trap). For this scenario, somewhere in a hallway near the attic door is good. (See the illustration on the next page.)

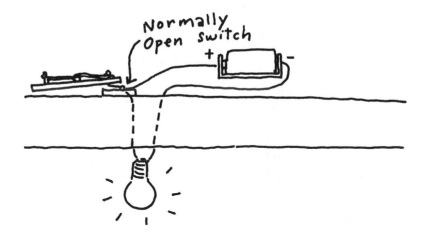

3   Use double-sided tape to mount the lightbulb holder and battery holder.

4   Next, route your wire to the spot where the mousetrap will be set.

5   Connect the wires to the N.O. alarm switch.

6   Place the fully set and baited mousetrap on top of the switch lever. This will keep the lightbulb from lighting until a mouse is caught and the trap moves off of the switch.

7   Keep your eyes open, and get ready to catch that varmint!

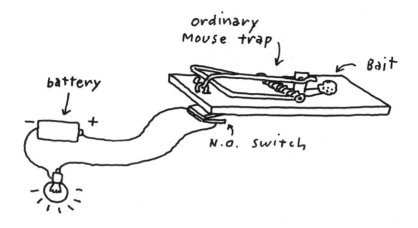

## Project 5

# The next step

What if the mouse is caught during the night when everyone is asleep? That's probably even more likely, so you had better make sure that the battery(ies) are well-charged because they might be on all night.

On the other hand, if you're willing to get out of bed and crawl up into the attic to get that mouse if it happens to get caught in the middle of the night, then you may want a fancier alarm system! You can substitute a not-so-loud siren and a blinking light with more parts and more power.

## Stuff you'll need

☞ Use all the base parts from the basic version: trap, wire, tapes, N.O. alarm switch, etc. You will add a parallel segment to your circuit—a siren similar to the ones used in smoke detectors. If you have an old smoke detector that no one wants (never, ever take parts out of a working smoke detector), you could even get yourself a siren for free! Otherwise, a trip to your local hobby/electronics store is in order.

❊ In this version, in place of the flashlight bulb, you can use a red, blinking light. Keep in mind that you might have to increase your battery size in order to power both for a long period.

## How to do it

Follow the steps from the earlier version. Substitute the alarm components as shown.

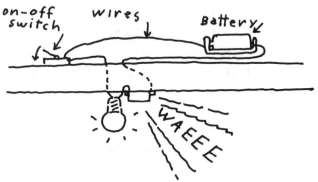

on-off switch    wires    Battery

WAEEE

A 9v battery will have to be used for this one.

![mouse drawing] ***A mouse about the house*** Common house mice use their senses of smell and hearing to find their way around. That means your trap and alarm setup doesn't have to look all that pretty because the mouse isn't noticing anyway! Its sense of smell is great at tracking down food or scents, so your bait will be important. Peanut butter is always good. Also, on many of the ultra-sticky traps, little scented seeds are included in the sticky part, which draw the mice to the trap.

House mice are well-tuned-in to high tones. You might find a way to keep mice away by transmitting a particular frequency that they don't like. It's worth a try. Maybe the next step in mousetraps is mouse prevention! After all, female mice can have litters of 6 to 11 mice in a period of 21 days. This means you could have a serious mouse problem in your house unless you get busy!

# Cool ideas

The same principle of using a normally open device to sense whenever some event has happened can be used in many other ways. Almost any object that can hold the lever arm shut on this type of switch is a good candidate. Doors, windows, TVs, CD players, and other objects can be set against the switch. With a lever arm that only requires a light load to shut it, most light objects (such as the mousetrap) will work also. Can you think of any other possibilities?

Besides the N.O. switch, there are other methods of sensing whether or not the mousetrap has moved. There are vibration sensors with adjustable levels of sensitivity, magnetic tape or foil—even magnetic switches can be used (of course, most mice aren't magnetic). You can experiment with any of these approaches. Remember, though, that the final action or result you desire at the siren or light (always on or always off) is the determining factor of which type of action you select for your sensor. Maybe you'll get your device patented if it is original enough!

Since there are so many different mousetraps on the market (everyone for years really has been trying to "build a better mousetrap"), you'll have to adapt your projects to the type of trap used. A lot of people are squeamish about actually killing a mouse. In fact, some traps confine the mouse and allow you, the trapper, to set it free—far away from your house. This is all the more reason to know as soon as possible that a mouse is caught. This project could be called the "living mousetrap alarm." The premise will be the use of either a "ultra-sticky"-type trap, or a plastic-cage trap with a one-way door. In either case, you can follow most of the steps from the original version to notify someone that a mouse is in the trap!

> *A patented idea* If you look at the many different mousetraps at the hardware store, you'll find many today with a *patent* number. Some will even say "Patent Pending." The inventor, once he or she had a "better mousetrap," registered the invention with the United States Patents Office so that it could not be copied. The lower the Patent number, the earlier it was invented. When the invention says "patent Pending," this means that the inventor wanted to begin marketing the product before it was registered.
>
> If you come up with a really great invention, won't you want to patent it, too? See the "suppliers" section in the back of this book to find out how.

## Ultra-sticky trap

In the case of the ultra-sticky trap, you can use the same normally open (N.O.) switch that we used with the spring trap. Almost every time, the entire trap will move off of the switch as the mouse tries to wiggle free, setting off the light alarm. Wire everything the same way.

## One-way door trap

If you use the one-way-door trap, your effort will be a little different. These traps work on the basis that once the mouse enters the trap, the door closes and it cannot get back out. There are air holes in it for the mouse to breathe, but it must be eventually set free. To sense that the door has been closed is relatively easy. You will need an electric drill, some hot glue, and an N.O. switch. This setup will be very sensitive because the door on these traps is usually very light and easily moved by a one-ounce mouse.

Some switches actually allow you to make sensitivity adjustments, and these might be a good idea for this kind of alarm. Check at the electronics store when you go to purchase one. Regardless of your choice of switches, once a mouse has gone near the door and actually touched it, you want to know. Simply attach the switch to the door so that it is triggered once the door moves. Finish the wiring scheme as you did in the original project and you're set! (See the illustrations on the next page.)

# Who needs a cat?

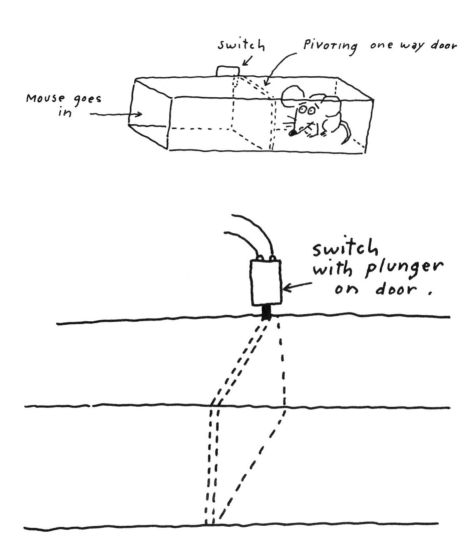

switch

Pivoting one way door

Mouse goes in

switch with plunger on door.

# Project **6**

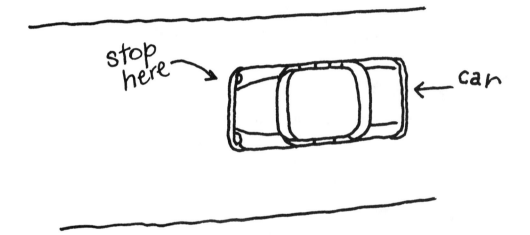

stop here →

← car

# Weight right there

**I**F YOURS IS LIKE MOST FAMILIES IN THIS COUNTRY, YOU probably have a garage full of junk! Bicycles, sleds, recycling bins, garbage cans, tools, mowers, toys, boxes and most other miscellaneous items end up in the garage. This makes parking the family car in the same garage a challenge (maybe even more of an adventure!).

What would your parents give to be able to park the car in exactly the right place, every time, without having to worry about bumping into your bike, the freezer, or the boxed-up Christmas decorations? Better yet, what would *you* give to rid yourself (if only for awhile) of being told to clean up the garage?

## Problem?

Space is so limited in your garage that it's practically impossible for your mom and dad to park the car in there, too, without bumping into something.

## Solution?

Rig up an alarm that will allow your parents to avoid every junk item in the garage while pulling into the same (safe) place every time.

 ## Science stuff

No doubt you have been in an automatic car wash with your parents. They press the secret number or insert the token and drive into the wash bay. How do they stop at the right spot? Usually there are two lights—a green light and a red stop light, right? But how do these lights know when your car is in the right position?

# Weight right there

The car-wash system of lights works on a pressurized-switch basis. The front tires of your car strike a plate that moves from the weight of the car. This allows the contacts to connect and send the electricity to the red stoplight, turning off the green light. Your parent brakes the car, puts it into park, and the car wash brushes can move all around your car, never hitting it (and they *never* hit the mirrors or antenna, do they? Ha!).

You are not making an automatic car wash out of your family garage, but you can use the same control theory for your project. Of course, there are also other ways to accomplish the same result, but that's the fun thing about controls, switches, and electronics . . . There are always other—and maybe even better— ways to do something.

Your project will make various assumptions about your garage. First, we'll assume that it is cluttered and that you must park the car precisely so that there will be room enough to walk around it or in front of it without crashing into something. Second, we assume that there will be some natural uneven-ness to your concrete garage floor. This is vital to the success of your project, but the good news is it's a pretty safe assumption. Almost every garage floor will have the uneven spot we need.

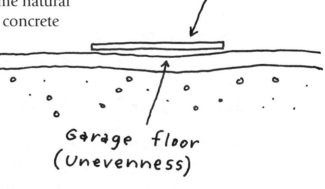

Metal Plate

Garage floor
(Unevenness)

# Project 6

The metal plate you use will also provide some unevenness. Are you now wondering why you need something uneven? Well, you're going to exploit that unevenness, your car's weight, and some self-adhesive metal foil to create your project.

## Stuff you'll need

- [ ] 1 concrete garage floor
- [ ] 1 metal plate, ⅛" thick by 12" wide by 24" long
- [ ] 1 9-volt battery
- [ ] 1 battery holder
- [ ] 1 9-volt high-intensity bulb
- [ ] 1 bulb socket
- [ ] 1 red, translucent plastic housing
      plenty of wire
- [ ] 24" of self-adhesive metal foil conductive tape (Radio Shack #49-502)
- [ ] 1 pair of self-adhesive foil connectors (Radio Shack #49-504)
      some electrical tape

*and* . . . one automobile with driver

## How to do it

1   First, find out from your parents where they actually want the car to stop. They might have to park it once for you so that you can mark the spot on the floor.

*More science stuff* Many security systems found in homes and in offices use the infrared photorelay approach. As you walk into the entryway of a business or walk down the hall, look around at about knee-level on the walls. You might just see a small, wall-mounted receiver/transmitter with what appears to be a red light. They are actually light-emitting diodes (LEDs) sending the infrared signal to the reflector, which sends the beam back. When the security system is armed (meaning that the beam is broken, the alarm will sound), the beam is broken by the legs or body of anyone walking by. When the security system is not armed, the beams can be broken and no alarm will sound. These infrared photorelay systems have typical limitations on effective distance, usually not more than 30 feet.

2    Take the metal plate and place it over the spot you marked. Stand on the plate to see if it will bend a little. If it bends, you're in good shape! That means that when the car goes over the plate, it will bend then, too, and make contact with the other foil strip.

3    Next, attach a 12″ strip of the self-adhesive metal foil conductive tape to the underside of the metal plate. You might have to adjust this length or cover some of the strip to avoid unintentional contacts. Hint: Make sure your plate is heavy enough so that it won't move from the desired location, making contact between foil strips difficult. If you can't get your hands on a heavy enough plate, consider securing it into place. Check with your parents to see what they will let you use for this (a good adhesive, concrete anchors, etc.) See the illustration on the following page.

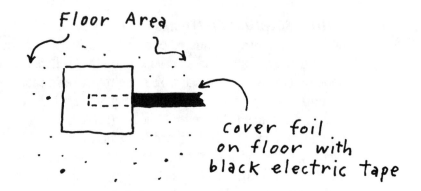

Floor Area

cover foil
on floor with
black electric tape

4   After placing a strip on the metal plate, you will now have to place a corresponding strip onto the floor. Remember, you are just trying to get an area between two foil strips to act as a "spring-like" switch.

5   Connect the strips to their respective foil connectors away from the car's path of travel. (You don't want the car or anyone else disturbing these connectors.)

Screw

Self sticking
connector

Foil

6   Determine where you want the lightbulb and housing to be placed, somewhere within direct, frontal view of the car driver. Mount all appropriate items: bulb socket, bulb, lens cover, and battery holder.

7   Run your wires from the connectors to the bulb, insert your battery, and get an adult to try it out. Hint: Tell your parents that as soon as they see the "red light" come on they should immediately coast a little bit forward so to allow the contact to be broken so the light will go out. If they don't do this, you will have to insert a switch to turn off for the light.

# The next step

Instead of stopping the family car on a metal plate by triggering a switch to turn on a light, you could use an infrared photorelay sensor system. Infrared photorelay systems and proximity sensors are a part of the technology known as *photoelectrics*. One version of this technology uses an infrared light. It's known as the *through-beam* photoelectric sensor because an object goes "through" the "beam" of light to set off the appropriate reaction. In the case of this project, a car would break the beam of light, set off the alarm or warning light, and signal to the driver to stop right there.

Light source

Through Beam Photo. electric sensor

Light detector

Beam is broken when object passes in front

car

Here's how it works: You get a one-piece transmitter-and-receiver package with a reflector plate (these are available at Radio Shack stores or other security-products stores). Some are battery-powered, while others require 120-volt ac power. By setting the transmitter/receiver on one side of the garage and the reflector plate on the other, an invisible beam will cross the garage space where the car is normally parked. When the car enters the garage and breaks the beam, the sensor will send a signal to your light. The driver will see the light come on and stop the car immediately.

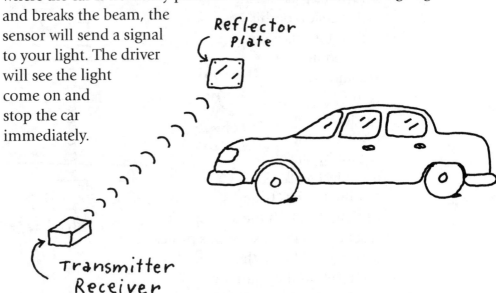

This version is simpler to install and set up, but it does cost more. The initial cost of the receiver/transmitter is more, but you also have to keep the beam powered continuously. Follow the same procedures for setting up the light and the wires to the light as you did in the original version. Of course, you will not have to find a metal plate or an unlevel spot on the garage floor, nor will you use foil contacts and electrical tape and wire to trigger the light for this version.

## Cool ideas

☞ There are tons of variations to this project. You are only limited to how much money your parents will allow you to spend!

✳ One variation you could try would be to use your house 120 vac power to run the red light. This will eliminate the need for a battery, holder, and flashlight bulb because you could use a conventional lightbulb. Still, try to get a red lens cover or even a red lightbulb (try the Christmas light collection!) so it will be easy to see.

✳ Another thing you might incorporate is a green light and red light system. When the garage door opens, the green light comes on. When the car hits the "right spot," the green light goes off and the red light comes on. Get creative!

✳ You might even use proximity sensors, which signal that an object is near. The *proximity sensor* uses the same light technology, but it operates on a principle of reflection rather than breaking a beam of light. Sometimes the "prox" sensor is referred to as the *reflective sensor*. These devices are probably cost-prohibitive right now, but they might not be in the near future. Besides, they are really cool!

Light source

Reflective
or
Proximity
Sensor

Light detector

# Project 7

# Out with intruders

THERE ARE ALL TYPES OF SECURITY SYSTEMS OUT THERE—from whole-house, silent types that alert a monitoring agency to those that just flash lights and make a lot of noise. These all cost a great deal of money. Usually, you have to pay a monthly fee to the monitoring agency, and before that, the installation costs can be staggering. Wouldn't it be awesome if you install a security system at your own house for a fraction of the cost? Surely your parents would be willing to listen to your plan if it saved them money . . . and it worked!

## Problem?

You want to feel safe all the time, especially when you're in your bedroom at night. Your parents assure you that the house is secure, and although they would love to install a security system, it costs way too much. What do you do?

## Solution?

You can install your own custom security system with the alarms of your choice and have some serious fun while doing it! Besides saving a lot of money, you might even invent a novel approach to an old problem.

## Plan ahead

First, think like a burglar. What places in your house are easy to get access to? Where is it the darkest? Is there a spot around the outside of your house where no neighbors can see? If any of the answers were obvious, you should concentrate in those areas.

Next, look at the doors and windows. What kind of alert do you want? Remember, the would-be burglar won't know how sophisticated your custom security is (or isn't). Many systems operate on the premise of simply "alarming" an intruder enough that they vacate the premises quickly because they don't know whether or not the police have already been called, what further security devices are in place, etc. Use this to your advantage in designing your own system.

You might not realize this, but there are plenty of available security products in your home right now. The siren-alarm portion of a smoke alarm can be used (Again, never, ever, *ever* take apart a working smoke detector . . . you need it to warn of fires!). Many of the lights in your home can be turned "on" on command. In addition, many personal computers are capable of dialing 911 or the police. All you have to do is use what's available and "exploit technology."

Make a visit to your favorite electronics store to check out the available security products. Tell a salesperson what you want to do, and ask lots of questions. You and your family don't need an expensive, elaborate security system that costs hundreds of dollars to install and carries a monthly monitoring fee.

Draw a floor plan of your house. Walk around the outside— especially after dark. On the floor plan, mark the locations that need to be secured. Next, map out your strategy. Do you want noise makers, lights, and other triggered options? Then present your illustrated plan to mom and dad. (See the illustration on the next page.)

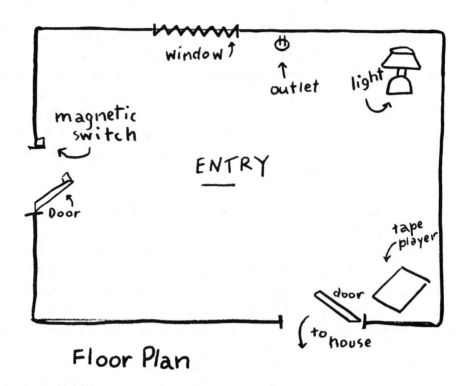

Floor Plan

The following project is not only professional-looking (to a burglar) but also fun to make. You can learn a lot about relays by putting this system together, but this is one you will absolutely have to discuss with your parents because it will involve working with 110-volt house electricity, if you go with the hard-wired version. Even if you go with the wireless version, you'll need mom or dad's permission (since that version is likely to cost a lot more!).

## Science stuff

What exactly is a *relay*, anyway? You're probably pretty familiar with the "relay race." In that type of a race, a fresh runner takes a baton and runs a *leg* (specified distance) of the race and then

you are intruding

passes the baton to the next fresh runner. Electrically, a relay performs a similar function. It takes an electrical signal from one source and mechanically exchanges that signal for another, usually of a different voltage.

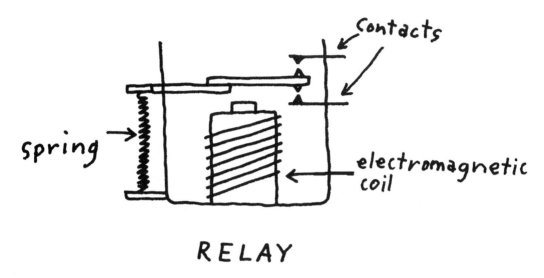

**RELAY**

A relay uses an electromagnet, springs, and stationary and movable contacts to trigger another powered circuit. In this way, only when the door is opened can you run all the 110-vac devices for your project. By combining several relays you can achieve many different control schemes. For control designers, "when in doubt, use relays!"

Because you will install a *magnetic switch* at the selected door, your alarms will be triggered when the door is forced open (when the system is "armed"). You will use multiple alarms. When the door is opened, a tape recording will play over and over in a loud, Darth Vader-like voice, "You are an intruder . . . the police have been notified . . . (pause) . . . You are an intruder . . . the police have been notified . . . !" Of course, the tape will play over and over, but someone in the house will have to take care of making that phone call to the police. (You could make it automatic by incorporating this idea into your existing system, later). In addition, a loud buzzer will go off in the garage area, creating even more noise and confusion for the intruder. Finally, a light will come on in a predetermined location, alerting you that someone has entered. With all this commotion, the intruder will leave immediately!

## Stuff you'll need

- ☐ 1 tape recorder/player
- ☐ 1 normally open (N.O.) magnetic contact switch (Radio Shack #49-533 or equivalent)
- ☐ 1 12-vdc plug-in relay (Radio Shack #275-218 or equivalent)
- ☐ 2 extension cords, one you can cut and the other long enough to reach another room near the garage
- ☐ 1 multiplug outlet strip (the kind used with computers and equipped with a switch)
- ☐ 1 lamp with lightbulb
- ☐ 1 110-vac to 12-vdc adapter (these are those power supplies that your family has accumulated over the years from answering machines, telephones, calculators, computers, etc.)
- ☐ 2 electrical outlets in the garage
- ☐ 1 4-20-vdc piezo buzzer (Radio Shack #273-059RJ or equivalent)
- ☐ soldering iron and some solder
- ☐ a plastic box

□ some electrical tape

□ a screwdriver

□ wire cutters/strippers

□ some 14-gauge wire or equal for the 110-vac wiring
□ some lighter-gauge wire (speaker-wire grade) for the 12-vdc wiring

## How to do it

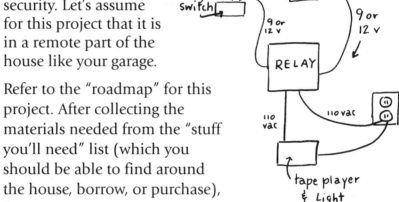

1 Find a door around your house that needs security. Let's assume for this project that it is in a remote part of the house like your garage.

2 Refer to the "roadmap" for this project. After collecting the materials needed from the "stuff you'll need" list (which you should be able to find around the house, borrow, or purchase), find your physical locations to mount your hardware.

3 Remember that part of this project will use 110vac house power. *Dangerous shocks can cause injury or even death. Always make sure you are not working with any "live" wires.* You should be able to do all your soldering, cutting, and taping of wires well before you apply any power. But to be safe, have an adult help!

4   Next, begin running the appropriate wires to the various locations. This way, you'll see how long each length will be and how and where you might conceal some wires (you want to hide as much of the hardware from the intruder as possible).

5   With the relay system, there are actually two circuits: the 12-vdc circuit and the 110-vac circuit. Finish the 12-vdc circuit first.

6   Using a screwdriver, mount the magnetic contact at the door.

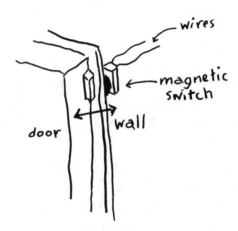

7   Connect all the low-voltage wires to and from the power supply and the switch. Then, solder the low-voltage wires to the relay contacts as shown. You also will be picking up 12-vdc power from this

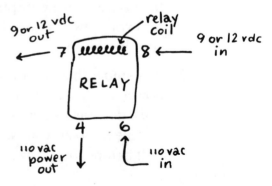

circuit for your electric buzzer. Mount the buzzer so that both the intruder and your house occupants can hear it.

**8** Before you wire the 110-vac wire to the relay, you must cut one leg of the extension cord to the multiplug outlet. Use wire cutters and wire strippers to do a good job! One part goes to one terminal on the relay and the other goes to another terminal on the relay and back out to the extension cord. You are, in effect, merely cutting and inserting the relay into the extension cord.

**9** Next, solder the 110-vac wires to the appropriate leads on the relay. Securely mount (electrical tape will work) the relay inside the plastic box or housing. Make sure you have left adequate means of egress for the wires.

**10** Mount or place the plastic box in an out-of-the-way location.

**11** Now you must decide where to hide the tape player and where the lamp is to turn "on."

**12** Once you have placed the tape player and the lamp, in your best Darth Vader voice, make your long, repeated recording. Remember—you're trying to scare off intruders, so make it sound "professional!"

**13** *Now*, and only now, you may plug in your power supply and the first extension cord. Plug in the tape player and lamp. Set the tape player to "play" and turn the lamp switch "on."

**14** Turn the switch at the multiplug outlet to "on" to arm your system.

**15** To test, make sure your garage door is unlocked, then go outside through another door in the house. Come in the secured garage door, and see what happens. If you did everything properly, you'll hear the buzzer go off first, then the tape will play and the light will be on elsewhere in the house. If these events happen, pat yourself on the back. Not only have you done a good job, but your family will be safer because of it.

*Did you know...* As we move toward the end of this century and into the next, technology is changing rapidly in the home security field. If we can't catch burglars, then we'll outsmart them! There are now "intelligent" systems being built into new homes. These systems allow home owners to program when an electrical outlet anywhere in the house comes "on" or turns "off." Through a central computerized programming station, the temperature of the house can be fully regulated, coffee can be automatically brewed at 7:00 a.m., and the house security system can be fully activated (complete with audio and video monitors). Video cameras, stereo systems, intercoms, and the like can be integrated into these automatic systems. A person could even dial up the system on their car phone and tell the system to turn on the oven, deactivate the security system, and run the furnace—all before they get home.

These systems are relatively expensive now, but costs are coming down. Special electrical wiring and special electrical outlets are required, which makes retrofitting an existing home difficult. You, the young control guru, could probably come up with many similar home automation projects—for a lot less money. Why not ask mom and dad today what they want automated?

## Cool ideas

Something mentioned earlier in this project was actually incorporating an automatic dialing system into the security alarm you just made. Instead of trying to bluff your intruder into thinking that a call was made, you could actually connect a telephone dialing device into the circuit, and trigger it to actually dial. This would make your alarm even more likely to deter an intruder, but the cost might be prohibitive.

Perhaps the single, coolest and cheapest security system you can make is something very simple, yet truly effective!! If you have a computer and a good printer, or if you can draw well, then you can start scaring off potential burglars without even wiring a single device. You can make up your own personal "warning" signs and labels. If you make them look authentic, you can tape them to your windows and doors so that people visiting will see that your premises are protected by a security system (even if it really isn't).

 # The next step

The previous hard-wired approach to this alarm system is relatively inexpensive. But today we have wireless controls available to us. If you are willing to pay a little extra for them, the wireless control schemes are really cool. For instance, with the previous project, instead of using a hard-wired relay, many lengths of wires, and a separate 12-vdc power supply, you could have bought a prepackaged, wireless system. It consists of a battery-powered switch with transmitter and a plug-in (to a 110-vac outlet) receiver module. These are similar to the Radio Shack Plug 'n Power security accessories. You can plug your tape player and lamp into this module and, when the door is opened, the transmitter sends the signal to turn "on" your alarms.

This is a common security control scheme, but it does cost more. On the other hand, it is initially easier to install because you don't have to route wires or solder any wire to the hard-wired relay. (See illustration on the next page.)

# Stay out of my stuff!

# Project 8

WE ALL HAVE OUR FAVORITE PERSONAL BELONGINGS.
And there are certain things that we absolutely, positively do not
allow anyone to move, touch, or borrow. But sometimes these
personal items *do* get disturbed, moved, and sometimes even
(heaven forbid) borrowed without our permission. Wouldn't it
be nice to know if someone has tampered with some of those
belongings?

Perhaps you have a nice CD collection, trading cards, or an
expensive set of stereo system components. Or maybe you want to
know if someone has been using your computer—unauthorized.
You might want to make these things "tamper-proof" so they're
protected from little brothers and sisters (or even older brothers
and sisters). Maybe you just want to protect something from
being stolen. Either way, you need a fool-proof, tamper-proof
system. For this project let's protect your portable CD player.

## Problem?

Seems someone is always messing with your prized possession,
your portable CD player. Of course, whenever you make this
statement to the family, no one knows what you're talking about.
You need a way to catch the little tamperer red-handed!

## Solution?

No, you don't have to double-lock your CD player and hide it
in a closet. Instead, make your belongings "tamper-proof" by
scaring the culprit away or by having proof that someone has
bothered your stuff!

KEEP
OUT

# Stay out of my stuff!

## Stuff you'll need

- ☐ 1 normally open tamper switch (Radio Shack #49-528 or equivalent)
- ☐ 1 9-volt battery
- ☐ 1 9-volt battery holder
- ☐ 1 low-voltage electric buzzer (Radio Shack # 273-059), to discourage the tamperer right away) *or* a flashlight bulb and socket (so you'll know, and the tamperer will not).
- ☐ some light-gauge wire
- ☐ wire cutters/strippers
- ☐ some electrical tape
- ☐ your CD player

## How to do it

1   First of all you need to be discreet. All wires, lights, and battery components will have to be hidden.

2   Place your CD player in an area where there are other things. This way the tamper switch will remain hidden better.

3   The tamper switch must be firmly seated to the surface near the CD player location.

4   Using your wire cutters/strippers, cut the wire to the length you feel is necessary. Cutting a length a little longer is always better than a little shorter! Then strip the wire to expose an adequate amount of conductor. The rule of thumb is to expose enough copper or aluminum conductor so that there will be enough to wrap around the terminal screw three-quarters of a turn. This should ensure a good, solid connection.

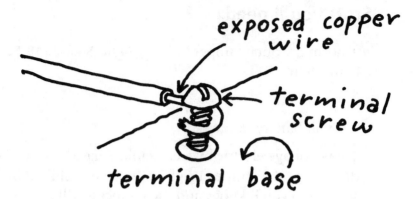

**5** Connect the wires to the tamper switch. Remember this is a normally open circuit, so whenever the plunger on the switch moves outward, the light or buzzer will turn "on."

**6** Mount the buzzer or light away from the tamper switch.

**7** Route all the wires.

**8** Next, you're ready to set the CD player against the tamper switch. You will note that the switch has a spring attached internally to the plunger. There is a certain amount of pressure that the CD player (or any object) will exert onto the switch and vice versa. You can adjust the amount of plunger to be depressed. In this way you can make your "trap" more or less sensitive. See the illustration on the next page.

**9** Insert your battery, and your trap is set.

KEEP
OUT

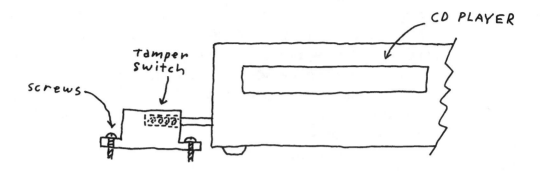

## Tips

Mount the buzzer up high, maybe above the door. This will help the sound travel farther. In the case of the lightbulb, hide it somewhere, like under your bed. Then whenever you go back into your room, you can immediately check to see if the light is "on" and prove that someone touched your CD player.

## Science stuff

Wire cutters and wire strippers are usually one in the same tool. For years, an electrician would have to use a knife to cut the casing around the wire conductor. Often, the conductor would get only partially cut and end up damaged or ripped off with the casing. The need for a common, safe utensil was there. The answer was the wire stripper/cutter shown here. It is perfect for anyone who has to do any wiring, and it will save time, reduce scrap, and lead to a lot less frustration.

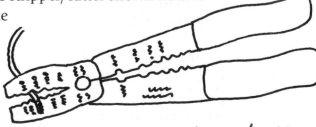

wire stripper/cutter

Tools often evolve because the need to do many functions with a single instrument is preferable. Besides, if a better cut of wire is made, a better electrical connection can be made. Electrical shorts and other problems are sometimes hard to find. A *short*, or *short circuit*, occurs whenever two wires that should never touch end up touching. The electricity flows extremely fast through this "path of least resistance." These are dangerous and bad situations, which can sometimes cause fires.

## Cool ideas

Obviously, the more elaborate the security and tamper-proof system, the more expensive and complex it will be. The more components you add, the more you also add a chance that a wiring error or loose connection can occur. This is the exact problem that faces most electricians in industry everyday. Keep your schemes simple! And if you do want to add that extra switch, wire, or circuit, just follow sound wiring procedures along the way and you should have no problems. Don't get careless when working with wires and electricity!

What other items in your room or around the house would you like to protect? How about your computer? Would you like to know if it has been used without your permission? If you are meticulous, you could set the tamper switch against your computer's mouse in such a way that if someone uses it, you would know (with the hidden light)!

The ultimate in security for this project would be to actually catch the thief red-handed! Could you tie a camera into the circuit so that it automatically takes a picture of the culprit once the object has been disturbed? A still photograph would be excellent—a VHS video recording with audio, even better!

KEEP
OUT

As we move into the 21st century, the electrical content of virtually every new invention will increase. Have you noticed how many battery-powered products have emerged? If it's not battery-powered, then it will most likely have a plug-in cable for your electrical outlet. Inventors are using electronics as they invent! For starters: Electricity is required for every microprocessor-driven device. As computers become more and more a part of our everyday lives, so do they become part of our future (and the thought process for inventing). Are you prepared for the next increase in electronic content to your future products?

 ## The next step

How about a compact, portable tamper-proof security system? A package with the tamper switch, battery, and light (or buzzer) all in one self-contained box. This would be the perfect thing to secure your items in your locker at school.

### Stuff you'll need

- □ tamper switch
- □ hot-glue gun
- □ small plastic box
- □ 9-volt battery
- □ battery holder
- □ some wire
- □ utility knife
- □ buzzer

## Project 8

### How to do it

**1** Following the illustration, cut a hole in the side edge of the plastic box so that the tamper switch plunger can be fitted through.

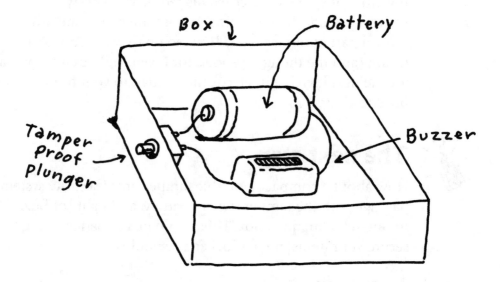

**2** Next, set the switch in place within the box so that the plunger fits out of the box and is operable.

**3** Attach some wire to both screw terminals on the back of the tamper switch. Glue the switch in place.

**4** Set the battery holder and buzzer within the box and glue each into place. (Note: if you find that it will be difficult to wire these devices when glued in place, then wire before gluing).

KEEP OUT

5   With all the components connected, insert the battery, and the buzzer should sound. Depress the tamper switch plunger, and the buzzer should stop. If the unit works in this fashion, close the lid and go find a valuable item that you want to protect. You might have to tape the plunger "down" in order to store or transport your portable protection unit. You could even take this unit to school (if you're allowed) and secure some things in your locker or desk. You might even be able to take orders for similar units and start a business! Check with mom or dad first!

KEEP OUT

# Turn on the lights—and everything else—from bed

THE PROJECTS IN THE BOOK HAVE PROBABLY STARTED your creative juices flowing. In fact, you're probably so into this control thing that your bedroom is starting to look like a maze of wires, gadgets, buttons, switches, and lights.

Wait a minute, here! Didn't you put all of this stuff together so you could organize things and make your life easier? Aren't you supposed to be in control? Then why does your bedroom look like it was decorated by Star Trek spiders? Maybe you should just disconnect everything and haul it off to the trash.

Not! What you need is something to put you back in control. Some organizer for all your switches and buttons and so on. A master control station, for the master of controls!

## Problem?

You've built all sorts of control gizmos and gadgets for your room, and they're all installed all over the place. Now you need a convenient, centralized place to control everything.

## Solution?

Build a custom-made operator control station (O.C.S.), and get back in control of your room!

For starters, we'll assume that you want to physically locate this box within arm's length of your bed. Secondly, you may want to begin with a larger than necessary box so that you can expand as time goes on! Lastly, we will need to find the proper, inexpensive materials either around the house or at our electronics store. This control box will make all the other kids on your block envious. They will most certainly ask you how you did it!

## Science stuff

Practically every machine, robot, and automated device has a control box. Robots need controls, and so do a lot of machines, like automobiles. Your family car has a dashboard with wiper, heater, air conditioning, and other controls—all at the touch of your parent's fingertips.

In factories, all those machines you see and hear running are controlled by someone. This someone is usually called the *operator*. The operator's control box is given a cooler name, the *operator control station*, or *O.C.S.* These factory versions have color monitors, touch screens, and lots of lights and pushbuttons. They also cost a lot. Your O.C.S. will be more practical.

### Stuff you'll need

You will need some appropriate box to house all your switches, lights, and labels (don't forget the labels—you might have to be reminded what a certain pushbutton is for, or somebody might have to turn something off when you're not around!). Make sure you find a large box, large enough that its depth can contain batteries, wires, etc., and also give you space to manuever within. On the outside, there should be plenty of surface area to mount several switches. When you're looking for your control box, consider that the box's material should be plastic or heavy cardboard so it's easier to cut and to mount your switches and pushbuttons. Finally, find a box that looks pretty good. It's going to be mounted in your room, after all, and neatness does count.

A great choice for a control box is an old plastic 5.25" floppy-disk case. It's plastic, easy to come by, and not really something anyone will miss, since 5.25" disks are on their way out (most computers today use 3.5" disks).

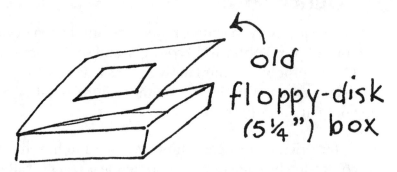

old
floppy-disk
(5¼") box

Next, determine what switches or pushbuttons you will want to mount. This project is going to house three: a *momentary* pushbutton for turning a dollhouse light on and off (sort of like an on-demand nightlight), a *maintained* switch to run a small radio, and—to be really cool—a mounted *remote control* switch to turn a fan on and off.

It pays to know your switches and buttons! A momentary pushbutton allows electricity to flow for the moment or moments that the pushbutton is pressed. A maintained pushbutton allows electricity to flow continuously until the button is pressed again or another maintained button is pressed to stop the flow. A *SPST*, or *single pole, single throw switch* has two terminals or connection points that switch one circuit on or off. An *SPDT*, or *single pole, double throw switch* switches one terminal (typically the middle one) between two other terminals. A *DPDT*, or *double pole, double throw switch* switches two terminals between two other pairs of terminals. (See the illustrations on the next page.)

# Turn on the lights—and everything else—from bed

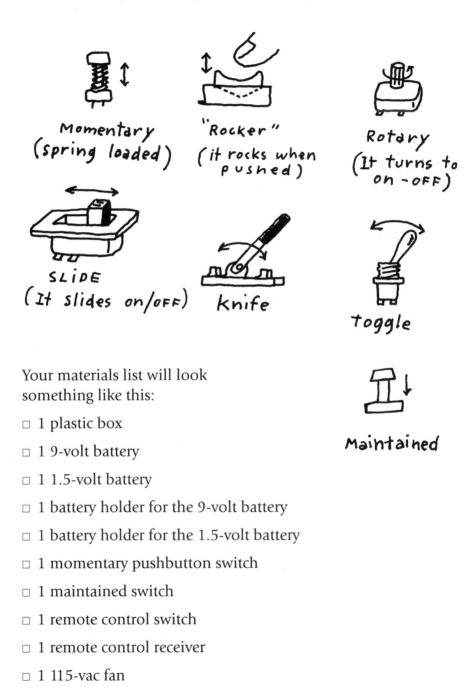

Momentary
(spring loaded)

"Rocker"
(it rocks when pushed)

Rotary
(It turns to on - off)

SLIDE
(It slides on/off)

knife

toggle

Maintained

Your materials list will look something like this:

- ☐ 1 plastic box
- ☐ 1 9-volt battery
- ☐ 1 1.5-volt battery
- ☐ 1 battery holder for the 9-volt battery
- ☐ 1 battery holder for the 1.5-volt battery
- ☐ 1 momentary pushbutton switch
- ☐ 1 maintained switch
- ☐ 1 remote control switch
- ☐ 1 remote control receiver
- ☐ 1 115-vac fan

## Project 9

- [ ] 1 9-volt-powered radio
- [ ] 1 1.5-volt light
- [ ] some electrical tape
- [ ] plenty of wire
- [ ] utility knife
- [ ] some double-sided tape

## How to do it

1. Lay out the switches and pushbuttons on the top surface of the plastic box. After marking the locations of each switch, cut out a hole at each spot, making sure that the switch will completely cover the hole.

2. Inside the box, locate the battery holders near their respective switches. Either tape or glue them into place. Feed the appropriate wires through to the switches on the outside of the box and connect them.

3. Do the same out through the bottom of the box with the wires going to the light or radio. Make sure you follow your diagram.

4   Before you make your final connections, make sure that you have enough wire to reach all necessary items: switch, battery, and light or radio. There should be enough wire to route and hide if possible.

5   Once the entire circuits are fully laid out, then you can make the final connections. Seat the switches into the control box.

6   Mount the wireless, remote-control transmitter (switch) on the front of the box.

7   Plug the receiver into the wall outlet, and plug the fan into the receiver. Turn on the switches to the radio, fan, and light. Now you will be able to control the on and off states of all these devices from your bed.

# The next step

To really jazz up your control box, why not try a super-duper version? You can really customize here, making the ultimate control box that fits your needs and budget perfectly. A quick walk through an electronics store will show you that there are a plethora of control gadgets out there. You can actually buy project enclosures made of molded plastic, aluminum, or steel. They come in all sorts of colors, sizes, and shapes, and many even have air slots, or *knockouts* that allow your wires to come in and go out, or all-purpose circuit boards. You have to first plan how many components you want to mount, and then select an enclosure that can fit them all.

***Remote controlled*** Remote-control stations are just OCSes that happen to be located away from the device they are controlling. The location is all relative. There are controls on a washing machine, dishwasher, and dryer. The convenient spot for these controls is on the front console of the machine, but they could certainly be repackaged and placed farther away (although the manufacturer of the product would probably void the warranty if you try this at home).

In special cases, however, controls on appliances and tools are located somewhere, sometimes so handicapped individuals can operate them more easily. If you want to count, every household in the country has between 7-10 controlled products or appliances within the home. Some are *analog*, such as push-to-start, hand timers, switches, or *rheostats*—devices that make an electric current weaker or stronger by changing the resistance in a circuit, etc. Other, newer units are digital.

All the remote controls we use for the television, CD players, VCRs, and so on are merely wireless, miniaturized control boxes. Many are digital, with solid-state electronics, microprocessors, and infrared technology replacing switches, relays, and wires from the older-style controllers. And someday, practically everything will be able to be controlled from your personal computer.

Always lay out the face of the control box on a full-scale sheet of paper. Once you have the final layout, determine what other items have to go on the inside (batteries, battery holders, wire, etc.). These all take up space. The switches and pushbuttons on top have a depth to them also. You should have a good idea on how tall, wide, and deep your control box has to be before you are ready to go to an electronics store and talk with a salesperson about how to outfit the size box you require with all the switches, buttons, and so on. Remember to take your planning sheet with you.

Once you get home, lay out the actual parts on the top of the enclosure and space them accordingly. Mark where each is to go and then start drilling and cutting as necessary. Route your wires, solder where necessary, and pull the external runs of wire out through the knockouts. Connect up to your controllable components, and you are now ready to energize!

## Cool ideas

At first these kinds of controls might seem lazy and unimportant, but remember that bit about inventions springing from someone's need. Maybe *you* don't really "need" a remote-control fan you can turn on and off from bed, but what about bed-ridden individuals, the sick, the elderly, the handicapped, and others who can benefit from devices such as these? For these purposes, a bedside remote control box more than makes sense.

Where else in your house could you use one? In the kitchen? In the garage? A central control station for tools or appliances might make a nice birthday present for mom or dad!. How about the home office? If you or a family member spends a good deal of time at the computer, maybe a remote-control box could be stationed right at the computer workstation.

# Glossary

**alternating current (ac)** An electrical current whose direction is changed 60 times per second. This is the common electricity found in most homes.

**amplitude modulated (am)** A type of radio wave that, by changing its strength, makes a change in the sound received at the radio.

**blind** Often associated with hunting, any device or method used to make something hidden from sight.

**carrier wave** A radio-frequency wave that carries information.

**circuit** The full and complete path of an electrical current, including all the components that affect that current.

**conductor** In electrical terms, the component that allows for the flow of electricity; the opposite of resistor.

**contacts** The junction of two electrical conductors that allows electrical current to flow whenever they touch.

**converter (ac to dc)** Sometimes called a power supply, this device simply takes 115 vac and converts it to some dc voltage (3, 6, 9, 12 vdc).

**cycle** Sometimes referred to as hertz, it is the measurement of frequency.

**direct current (dc)** An electrical current that flows in one direction continuously. This is the common electricity found in most batteries.

**electricity** A form of energy consisting of positively and negatively charged particles, such as protons and electrons, that interact with one another in magnetic, chemical, or inductive situations.

**electromagnetism** The principle, largely developed by Michael Faraday, whereby a stronger magnetic field is created by passing a lesser magnetic component through the region of a current-carrying conductor. This is the basic premise for most ac and dc motor operation.

**electronics** The science that involves the control of electricity and electrons, such as with computer and control equipment.

**frequency** The number of times something is repeated in a given period of time. As for sound, electrical, and radio waves, the number of times the wave is repeated is measured in cycles (or hertz) per second.

**frequency modulated (fm)** A type of radio wave that, by changing the number of "vibrations" per second, changes the sound received by the radio.

**gauge** The standard measure of the thickness or diameter of wire.

**hertz (Hz)** Sometimes referred to as cycles, it is the measurement of frequency.

**infrared** Rays of light that are just beyond red in the spectrum, which cannot be readily seen and can produce heat deep within an object.

**insulator** For electrical wires: glass, porcelain, or various plastics that will not allow current to flow; the casing around copper or aluminum wire.

**integrated circuit (IC)** A multilayer silicon wafer encapsulating many semiconductor devices such as diodes and transistors.

**knockouts** The holes in electrical equipment that allow wires and conduit in or out are covered by these plastic or metal pieces.

**light-emitting diode (LED)** Diodes allow electricity to flow in one direction only, and LEDs are made from a semiconductor material that provides energy bands of different wavelengths, thus producing a red or green color.

**leads** The terminal ends of insulated electrical conductors.

**maintained pushbutton** Electricity will flow continuously once this pushbutton has been depressed and will not stop flowing until another pushbutton, or this one, is pressed again.

**microwaves** Electromagnetic waves used in microwave cooking that are generated by a magnetron at 2,450 MHz.

**momentary pushbutton** Electricity will flow for the moment or moments that a pushbutton is depressed.

**motion sensors** Any device that can detect movement and then turn something on or off.

**network** An interconnected system of components all tied together by typically interlinking lines of wire and cable.

**Ni-Cd battery** A rechargeable battery made from nickel and cadmium.

**nonconductive** In electrical terms, that which does not allow for the flow of electricity.

**normally closed (N.C.)** A switch when first applied to an electrical circuit allows current to flow. When the switch is triggered, the circuit opens.

**normally open (N.O.)** A switch when first applied to an electrical circuit allows no current to flow; the circuit is open. When the switch is triggered, the circuit is complete and the current can flow.

**oscillate** Whenever a rigid body pivots to and fro or back and forth in a repeated fashion.

**operator control station (O.C.S.)** A housing that encloses pushbuttons, lights, switches, associated wiring, and any other component necessary for control from that housing. These stations can be made from metal or plastic, can be big or small, and can even house color monitors and computers.

**patent** An official document issued by the government giving an inventor the exclusive rights to his or her invention for a given period of time.

**photoelectrics** The technology that uses light energy, typically an infrared beam, in any electrical circuit to control turning devices on or off; sometimes called an infrared photorelay sensor.

**photovoltaics** The technology that allows electricity to be produced directly from sunlight.

**power supply** The energy source needed for most electrical circuits to run motors, lights, or other devices. This energy is ac or dc and low or high voltage, depending on the device being powered.

**proximity sensor** Sometimes called a reflective sensor, this photoelectric sensor uses a beam of infrared light that has "bounced" or reflected off of an object to detect its presence.

**radio waves** Electromagnetic signals transmitted and received at certain frequencies.

**receiver** The component that accepts and decodes signals from a transmitter.

**relay** A device that takes an electrical signal and energizes an electromagnetic switch which connects the two contacts of another circuit, thus completing it.

**remote control** Being able to turn a non-local device on or off from a local position. This also can involve more than just on and off circuits (faster, slower, up, down, etc.). This control scheme can be accomplished with hard wiring or by wireless means.

**rheostat** A device that makes an electric current weaker or stronger by changing the resistance in a circuit.

**short or short circuit** Electricity will take the path of least resistance, and a short circuit is an undesirable route taken by electrical current in a circuit. Typically, the short is dangerous to humans or equipment because high currents exist.

**shortwave** The HF or high frequency range of radio waves, 3-30 MHz.

**switch** A device used to turn something on or off by opening and closing an electrical circuit.

**technology** The science and study of processes, engineering, and application in related fields of knowledge.

**terminal** The point at which a wire is connected.

**through-beam sensor** A type of photoelectric sensor that emits an infrared beam of light to a dedicated receiver. If the beam is broken, something is turned on or off.

**transformer** An inductive device, usually made of iron with copper or aluminum coils, used to match voltages in an electrical circuit.

**transmitter** The component that sends a signal; typically requires a power supply.

**wire** That media, usually copper or aluminum, by which electrical energy is carried from one device to another.

**wireless** A system using radio or light waves to transmit signals from one device to another.

# Suppliers

AMERICAN SCIENCE AND SURPLUS
3605 Howard Street
Skokie, IL 60076
(708) 982-0870
(800) 934-0722 (fax)
*Lots of neat stuff for the hobbyist; not too expensive.*

DIGI-KEY CORPORATION
701 Brooks Avenue South
Thief River Falls, MN 56701-0677
(800) 344-4539
*Electronic stuff from 3M, Panasonic, AMP, etc.*

EDMUND SCIENTIFIC COMPANY
101 East Gloucester Pike
Barrington, NJ 08007-1380
(609) 547-8880
*Should have everything you will need; good technical support.*

# Turn on the lights from bed

JDR MICRODEVICES
1224 S. Bascom Avenue
San Jose, CA 95128
(800) 538-5000
*Electronic parts catalog supplier; good prices and service*

NEWARK ELECTRONICS
4801 N. Ravenswood Avenue
Chicago, IL 60640-4496
(312) 784-5100
*Electronics distributor; call or write for catalog and local office.*

RADIO SHACK
A Division of Tandy Corporation
P.O. Box 2625
Fort Worth, TX 76113
(800) THE SHACK
*They have answers to your electrical questions—and most of the hardware, too!*

W.W. GRAINGER CORPORATION
5959 West Howard Street
Chicago, IL 60648
(312) 647-8900 or (800) CALL WWG
*Great source for tools, motors, power transmissions, and electrical supplies; hundreds of branch locations across the U.S.*

*NOTES:*

**1.** Of course the emphasis of this book is to be RESOURCEful yourself! Check your own home first. Look inside of discarded products—take 'em apart! USE THE FREE OR CHEAP STUFF, FIRST!

**2.** Also, the local hardware store has many, many items...just ask. There are also many local scientific and technology stores. Look in the phone book.

**3.** And, if by chance you need to get a patent for your invention:

UNITED STATES PATENT AND TRADEMARK OFFICES
Washington, DC 20231

# Index

# *About the author*

Robert Carrow lives in Harmony, Pennsylvania. He travels extensively, providing motion and control solutions for industrial applications and machines. He is an automation engineer, the father of two future inventors, and the author of several papers and books.

# Contest Rules

**To Enter:** You may enter at any time and you may submit multiple entries. You must use the entry form in this book, which may be photocopied. Fill out the form completely and submit it with a nonreturnable photograph of your project. If you are one of the five finalists selected by the panel of judges, you will be contacted to submit your project. Failure to submit your project if you are a finalist will result in disqualification.

**Eligibility:** Anyone ten through sixteen years of age may enter, excluding employees of McGraw-Hill and their dependents. A parent or guardian over the age of 21 must sign on the Signature Line.

**How a Winner Is Selected:** A panel of judges, each of whom is active in the field of industrial technology, is selected by Learning Triangle Press, an imprint of McGraw-Hill, or its representatives. This panel determines the five finalists and the winner. The judges' decision will be based on practicality, creativity, and originality and will be final.

**Prizes:** A prize of U.S. $500 will be awarded annually. All entries received from June 1 of one year through May 31 of the following year compete for the same award.

**Winner's List:** For the name of the winner in any year, send a self-addressed, stamped envelope, between August 15 and December 15 of the year in question, to SciTech Sweepstakes, Learning Triangle Press, Associate Director of Marketing, 11 West 19th Street, New York, NY 10011.

All federal, state, and/or local rules and regulations apply. Void where prohibited by law. Winners are responsible for any and all taxes associated with their acceptance of any prize. Sponsor is not responsible for misdirected or illegible entries. In the event that any winners fail to accept their prizes or fail to meet the eligibility requirements, the unawarded prizes will be awarded to a runner-up contestant. Winner will be required to sign a release and affadavit that, among other things, will permit use of winner's name and a description of the winning entry in publicity materials.

**Win $500 CASH!**

*Learning Triangle Press*
## SciTech Sweepstakes
### Official Entry Form

Name _____ Age _____

Address _____

_____

City _____ State _____ Zip _____

Country _____

Telephone ( ____ ) _____

Parent or guardian must sign Signature Line:

Parent or guardian's name _____

Signature _____

Attach additional sheets if necessary to answer the following questions.

Describe your invention.

_____

_____

_____

_____

_____

_____

_____

What pages of the book were most helpful?

_____

_____

Which projects from the book did you build?

_____

_____

What did you learn?

_____

_____

_____